AF515523

# Passport, Pain, and Power

*From Dreams to Strength*

By

**Ashish Kejriwal**

***Passport, Pain, and Power***



ISBN: 978-93-5592-649-4

# Dedication

This book is dedicated to every soul who carried dreams heavier than their resources.

To those who stood in visa lines with hope in their eyes and fear in their hearts.

To those who left home not because they wanted to, but because staying meant suffocating their potential.

It is for the ones who were judged by their accent before their ability,
who were measured by their passport instead of their character,
and who learned that pain is not the opposite of power—it is often the birthplace of it.

Most of all, this book is for those who kept going when quitting felt logical, who chose growth over comfort, and who turned silent struggles into quiet strength.

If you see yourself in these pages, know this:
you were never weak—you were becoming.

# Acknowledgements

This book was shaped by distance, discipline, and moments that did not feel meaningful at the time.

I owe everything to my family, who gave me roots strong enough to walk away and faith strong enough to let me return changed. Their sacrifices are written between every line.

To my wife, Shivangi—thank you for seeing the man behind the ambition. For grounding me when I was drifting and reminding me that progress does not have to come at the cost of presence. This journey carries your quiet strength.

To the mentors, colleagues, and strangers who crossed my path—some offered guidance, others resistance. Both sharpened me. Growth rarely arrives without friction.

To those who doubted me, underestimated me, or dismissed me—your skepticism clarified my direction more than encouragement ever could.

And to the version of myself who once felt invisible, uncertain, and expendable—this book exists because you kept going. You endured the weight so that something meaningful could rise from it.

This story belongs to anyone who has ever chosen persistence when quitting felt reasonable.

# Table of Contents

# Preface

Embarking on a journey—whether across oceans or deep within ourselves—is a universal experience that binds us as human beings. *Passport Pain and Power* invites you to walk alongside Aaryan, a young dreamer whose heart carries both trepidation and hope as he leaves the familiarity of his homeland in search of something greater. This book is not merely the story of one man's pursuit of success; it is a reflection of struggle, resilience, and transformation—threads that connect us all, regardless of where we come from or where we are going. It is an invitation to confront fear, embrace the uncertainty of change, and redefine identity while navigating the vast, unpredictable seas of life.

As you step into Aaryan's world, you may find moments that echo your own experiences. Have you ever felt like an outsider in an unfamiliar place? Have you questioned a life-altering decision, wondering whether you chose the right path? Perhaps you have held tightly to the traditions of your past while feeling the quiet pull of new ideas that challenge your sense of comfort and belonging. Within these pages, Aaryan's journey unfolds not only as a story of migration and adaptation, but as a deeply personal exploration of identity—its fragility, its resilience, and its capacity for growth.

In writing this book, I sought to capture the essence of transformation: how the pain of leaving behind what we know can become a catalyst for profound growth. Too often, we view our struggles as barriers that hold us back, failing to recognize that they can also become our most powerful teachers. Aaryan learns this truth through lived experience. He faces language barriers that isolate him, cultural shocks that challenge his sense of belonging, and moments of vulnerability that strip away pretense and reveal his inner strength. Through his eyes, we witness a gradual awakening—a strength forged not by the absence of fear, but by the courage to confront it.

The journey from departure to transformation is never linear. It is a winding path marked by uncertainty, loss, small victories, and unexpected joy. Each chapter represents a stage in Aaryan's evolution, illustrating the power of resilience and the human capacity to redefine oneself. In *Departure*, we experience the ache of leaving home and the longing for what lies ahead. In *Transition*, we confront the raw realities of adjustment—an unfamiliar world that provokes anxiety while quietly nurturing hope. In *Transformation*, we witness moments of breakthrough, where struggle gives way to self-acceptance and empowerment.

At its heart, *Passport Pain and Power* is also a story about community. Along his journey, Aaryan encounters individuals who embody resilience in their own ways: his mother, whose unwavering love anchors him to his roots; Ravi, whose mentorship helps him navigate unfamiliar terrain; Leila, whose friendship reveals the beauty of cultural exchange; and Fatima, whose guidance ignites his passion for language. These relationships serve as reminders that no journey is undertaken alone. Human connection becomes a lifeline, balancing hardship with compassion and reinforcing the strength found in shared experience.

As you turn each page, I invite you to reflect on your own journey. What challenges have shaped you? What dreams remain dormant, waiting to be realized? We all possess the capacity to rise from adversity, yet we often underestimate the strength that already resides within us. Through Aaryan's story, I hope you will recognize pieces of your own narrative and see that resilience is often born through vulnerability.

In the spirit of exploration and connection, I encourage you to share your reflections and insights. The journey toward self-discovery is richer when experienced together, and communities are built through shared stories. Through conversations, discussions, and engagement beyond these pages, my hope is to foster connections that transcend borders and speak to the universal nature of growth and transformation.

*Passport Pain and Power* seeks not only to inspire readers to pursue their dreams, but also to embrace the difficult, transformative process that accompanies them. Beneath struggle lies an invitation—to awaken to the fullness of life and to recognize that our most challenging moments often lay the foundation for our greatest achievements. So, as you begin this journey with Aaryan, I invite you to lean into discomfort, to honor the complexity of change, and above all, to discover the power of resilience within yourself.

Welcome to a story of hope.

Welcome to a celebration of courage.

Welcome to *Passport Pain and Power*.

CHAPTER ONE

# A Leap of Faith

Aaryan stood at the doorway of his family home, feeling a mix of nostalgia and unease. This house was more than bricks and mortar; it held his childhood, his family's laughter, and the scent of spices that always seemed to linger in the kitchen. Each corner carried a memory, the faded artworks he had painted as a child, the worn sofa where he spent evenings listening to his mother tell stories of brave heroes.

He pressed his hand against the cool door frame, trying to steady the fluttering in his chest. Leaving would mean stepping away from all of it, every smell, every sound, every small comfort. Yet, the decision waiting beyond these walls promised something greater.

For nights, he had pored over travel brochures, imagining city streets alive with possibility. Skyscrapers gleamed like beacons of opportunity, and he pictured himself walking among them, free to shape his own future. His parents had struggled to keep their dreams alive under the weight of daily life. He hoped his journey might be different. Still, the thought of leaving behind the familiar tugged at him, a quiet but relentless pull.

Stepping into the sunlit street, Aaryan squinted against the brightness. Children laughed nearby, a vendor called out over the clatter of passing trams, and the smells of cooking drifted from open windows. Each ordinary detail seemed suddenly charged with meaning, pulling at him and reminding him of what he would leave behind.

He reminisced about his mother's words from last night. "Promise me you'll stay true to yourself," she said softly. Her words, gentle but heavy with love, echoed in his mind. He had nodded, forcing a small smile. He didn't want her to see the fear twisting in his stomach.

What if he failed? What if the foreign land wasn't what he imagined? But still, he had to try. He took a deep breath, letting the sun warm his face, and stepped forward. Each step carried him further from home, yet also closer to the life he had always dreamed of.

Gathering strength to counter his fears and doubts, he went back inside to book a cab.

His parents stood waiting, both of them pretending to look occupied, though their eyes kept drifting toward him. His father adjusted the same strap on Aaryan's bag again and again, tightening it, loosening it, then smoothing it down as if it might suddenly slip away. His mother folded and unfolded the edge of her dupatta, straightened papers that were already aligned, checked the time on her phone without really seeing it. No one spoke. Words felt dangerous, like they might crack something open that none of them could afford to break. Aaryan understood then that the silence was an act of love. If they spoke, their voices might tremble, and if their voices trembled, his resolve might falter. So they stayed busy with nothing at all, holding themselves together long enough to let him go.

Then, Aaryan cleared his throat and said, "It's here," and those simple words made something shift in the air, a quiet acceptance that the moment they had all been avoiding had finally arrived.

They walked with him to the gate, each step slow and measured as if delaying the inevitable might somehow change it. His mother adjusted the collar of his shirt even though it was already straight, her fingers lingering a second too long before letting go. His father picked up the bag for a moment, tested its weight, then handed it back with a firm nod. Aaryan took a slow breath, memorizing their faces, the familiar creak of the gate hinge, the scent of morning air warming under the sun. When the cab pulled up to the curb, he offered a small smile and said, “Let’s go.”

After placing his luggage in the back, they all sat in the cab. Though they smiled, the quietness in the cab spoke loudly. Their eyes told the truer story, one of pride tangled with worry and reluctant hope.

It was an awkward 30 minutes for a family that never sat together without laughter and chatter. For Aaryan, the journey to the airport felt unreal, each mile taking him farther from the place he had always called home and deeper into the unknown. Aaryan stole glances out of the window, trying to hold every sight in his mind. The familiar storefronts glowed in bright colors, and the scent of chai mixed with the earthy aroma of the street market, a perfume that seemed to define the streets he had grown up on. He was noticing the small details, the beauty of life around him. The things that looked mundane were now very special. A child chasing a stray dog, the flutter of laundry hung across narrow balconies, the worn wheels of a bicycle rattling over uneven pavement. He soaked each of these sights deep into his memory, as if storing them for comfort in the isolation.

His chest felt tight as the car slowed at a red light, and for a moment he wished the signal would never turn green. His fingers pressed into his jeans, restless, while his parents sat quietly beside him, their presence heavy and reassuring at the same time. This was not a temporary goodbye. He could feel it in the way his throat burned and his eyes lingered on every corner they passed. The city did not know he was leaving, yet everything around him seemed to pause, as if asking him to stay. He realized then that home was not just a place he could return to with a ticket. It lived in habits, in faces, in the rhythm of daily life he had never questioned before. As the car moved forward again, Aaryan understood that crossing borders would change him in ways he could not undo, and that carrying his homeland within him would be the only way to survive what lay ahead.

When he arrived at the airport, the contrast between home and the unknown struck him sharply. Travelers surged past, rolling suitcases and hurried footsteps forming a tide that made him feel like a solitary island in the middle of a vast, restless ocean. He paused, taking in the polished floors and high glass ceilings, the hum of announcements weaving through the space, the bright lights reflecting off every surface. It was overwhelming, yet exhilarating.

When they reached the point where only passengers could continue, the pace of their steps slowed. His mother wiped her eyes with the back of her hand, trying to hide the movement but failing. He placed his bag down and took a moment to look at both of them, really look, memorizing their faces framed by the bright airport lights.

His mother stepped forward first. "If anything feels wrong, you call. You message. You do not keep things inside," she said, her voice cracking despite her efforts to steady it. She touched his cheek with trembling fingers, and he felt them linger as if she feared that letting go would make him disappear.

"I will," he said softly. "I promise. I'll take care of myself." The words came out steadier than he expected, though his throat tightened painfully.

She blinked quickly, trying to hold back the tears gathering in her eyes. "And you eat properly. Not just bread and tea. I know how you get when you are busy."

He let out a small breath of laughter. "I know. I'll eat real food."

"I mean it," she insisted. "You forget meals. You stay up all night. Do not do that there. Your body is all you have. You must respect it."

"I will. I'll try harder. I'll be responsible."

She nodded, but her lips trembled. "And tell me when you reach. Even if it is late. Even if you are tired."

"I will. You will hear from me the moment I land."

She took his hands in hers. "You are going far. I know you want this, and I want it for you too, but it scares me." Her voice thinned. "You were so small when you first held my hand and refused to let go. I keep seeing that little boy when I look at you."

He swallowed. "I am still holding on, just in a different way."

Her breath hitched, and she looked down at their joined hands. "You grew so fast. I am happy, but my heart is heavy." She looked back up at him. "Will you miss us?"

"More than you think," he said, a shaky smile forming. "More than I can even put into words."

She brushed a strand of hair from his forehead. "Do not forget where you come from. Do not forget who you are."

"I won't. I carry it with me."

She took a deep breath, trying to steady herself again. "And if it ever becomes too hard, do not pretend you are fine. You tell me. You tell us. There is no shame in needing help."

"I'll be honest with you," he said, looking into her eyes. "I know I pretend sometimes, but I'll try not to."

She nodded slowly, tears finally spilling over. "You are my child. No distance can change that."

He gently wiped the tears from her cheeks. "I'll make you proud."

"You already have," she whispered. "You always have."

They stood for a quiet moment, their foreheads almost touching, neither wanting to pull away first.

After a while, Aaryan's father stepped forward. He didn't say anything at first. Instead, he reached out and adjusted the strap of the bag on his son's shoulder, checking the buckle twice even though it didn't need checking. A small habit, familiar and comforting. His eyes glistened, but he blinked slowly, steadying himself.

"You are ready," his father said at last. "You worked hard for this. Do not doubt yourself now."

"I know," he replied, though doubt hovered inside him like a restless shadow. "Thank you. For everything."

His father nodded once, firm but quiet. "Go on then."

There was a brief pause, the kind that stretches between hearts when none of them wants the moment to end. He took one last look at them. His mother was wiping away tears, and his father stood tall, but sadness was etched into every line of his face.

"Goodbye," he said.

With a final, lingering glance, he turned toward the line, the sound of his family's soft crying fading behind him as he stepped forward through the terminal gate.

Aaryan pulled his passport from his pocket, the crisp pages proof that he had never stepped beyond the borders of the land he was born in. He traced the front page absentmindedly, feeling its significance more now than ever. The immigration counter loomed ahead, a checkpoint between the known world and the life he was about to step into. His heart thumped faster, a mix of nerves and hope swirling together.

"Aaryan," he whispered under his breath, as if saying his name aloud could steady him, could remind him of the boy who had grown into a man capable of taking this leap. He could almost hear his father's stories of distant lands, the tales of challenges faced and triumphs won, and he imagined his mother's smile, warm and proud, waiting to hear the stories he would one day tell. He rubbed the back of his neck and shifted his weight from one foot to the other, small gestures that reflected his attempt to contain the storm of emotions inside him.

As he moved through the security checks, the harsh lights overhead flickered intermittently, making the entire space feel tense and watchful. The hum of scanners, the shuffle of shoes across polished floors, the clipped voices of officers all pressed in on him. How would he manage the new language, the cultural habits, the routines that would feel unfamiliar at every turn? A small knot of anxiety twisted in his chest, and he swallowed hard, tasting it bitter on his tongue. What if the new country swallowed him whole, leaving him lost among strangers?

Fortunately for him, his fear of being held at the immigration counter was behind him. After thorough checking and a couple of questions from the immigration officers, he was cleared. Now he waited for his flight.

After some minutes of waiting, the final boarding call echoed through the terminal. He paused at the gate, taking a slow, deliberate breath, feeling the lump in his throat grow heavier. When he stepped onto the plane, the engines were rumbling to life beneath him.

The cabin felt colder than he expected, filled with unfamiliar sounds and soft instructions spoken over the speakers. Aaryan slid into his seat and traced his fingers along the armrest, grounding himself in the reality of where he was. As the plane began to move, his heart thudded hard against his ribs. The runway blurred past the window, and when the wheels finally lifted, his stomach dropped and his breath caught. He watched the ground pull away, the city shrinking into a scatter of lights, and with it, the life he had always known.

As the plane climbed higher, he felt the thrill of possibility rise alongside the unease. Every lesson from home, every story, every small act of care, became something he carried inside him, a guide through the unfamiliar. He straightened in his seat, hands tightening around the armrest as determination steadied him. The city he would reach was unknown, and the culture, the people, the streets, all would test him. Yet he resolved to meet each challenge, to shape his future with deliberate steps.

CHAPTER TWO

# Stranger in a Strange Land

The plane door opened, and sound rushed in before anything else. Voices overlapped, quick and sharp, rising and falling in rhythms Aaryan could not follow.

"Move up, please."

"Tickets out."

"Watch your step."

The words came from different directions, blending into one another as passengers flowed past him. He hesitated at the end of the jet bridge, tightening his grip on his bag strap while someone brushed his shoulder.

"Sorry," the man muttered without slowing.

Aaryan stepped aside, letting the current pass. He stood still for a moment, listening. Laughter burst nearby. A phone rang. An announcement crackled overhead, its words swallowed by echoes before he could catch more than a few familiar syllables. He followed the signs only after watching three others move in the same direction.

Inside the terminal, the lights were brighter than he expected. He blinked, adjusted his jacket, and scanned the crowd. People walked fast, eyes forward, confident in where they were going. He matched their pace, though his steps lagged half a second behind.

At baggage claim, the carousel jolted to life with a metallic groan. Suitcases thumped onto the belt, one after another. He leaned forward, scanning tags and colors, then frowned when the belt looped again without his bag.

Aaryan approached the counter.

“Excuse me,” he began. His voice sounded smaller than usual. “My luggage did not come.”

The woman behind the counter looked up. “Did you file a claim already?”

He paused. “I… no. I just arrived.”

She leaned slightly forward. “Was it a direct flight or a connection?”

“A connection,” he answered, then hesitated. “I think.”

She nodded as if this was expected and pulled a thin stack of papers from a drawer. “Okay. Then we start here.” She slid a form toward him. “Fill this out. Tag number goes here. You will need the address where you’re staying.”

He stared at the paper. His eyes moved over the lines, but the words blurred together. The noise around him felt louder now. Wheels of suitcases rattled across the floor. A child cried somewhere behind him. An announcement echoed from the ceiling, too fast for him to understand.

“Address,” he repeated, more to himself than to her.

She tapped the paper with her finger. “Right here.”

“Yes. Okay,” he said, nodding, though his hand hovered uncertainly above the page. He reached into his pocket and pulled out his phone, unlocking it slowly. The screen showed a message from his cousin with an address he had copied earlier. He read it once. Then again. He began to write, carefully forming each letter as if speed might cause a mistake.

Behind him, someone cleared their throat. Another person shifted their weight. He felt the pressure but kept his eyes down. When he finished the line, his handwriting looked cramped and uneven.

The woman glanced at the form. “Tag number?”

He looked up. “Sorry?”

“The baggage tag. From your boarding pass.” She mimed tearing a small sticker.

“Oh. Yes.” He fumbled through his passport, papers slipping slightly from his grip. His boarding pass was folded too many times. He unfolded it, smoothing it against the counter. His eyes searched the numbers.

She waited, expression neutral.

“This?” he asked, pointing.

She leaned closer. “No. That’s the flight number. The tag is longer.”

He nodded again, embarrassed, and turned the paper around. After a moment, he found it. “Here.”

She wrote something on her computer. “Bag color?”

“Color?”

“Yes. Black, blue, gray?”

“Black,” he said quickly. Then paused. “With… a red strap.”

She typed. “Hard or soft case?”

“Soft,” he answered, though he was not fully sure. He hoped he was right.

“Brand?”

He blinked. “Brand?”

She exhaled softly, not annoyed, just tired. “Any name on the bag?”

“No name,” he said. “Just… old.”

She nodded. “Okay. When did you last see it?”

“At… before,” he said, searching for words. “Before last plane.”

“At the connection airport?”

“Yes. Yes.”

She looked at the screen again. “Your bag may still be there. Or it may arrive on the next flight.”

“When?” he asked.

“Could be today. Could be tomorrow.” She handed him a small slip of paper. “This is your claim number.”

He took it carefully. “They will call?”

“Yes. Or email.” She looked at him. “Do you have a local phone number?”

He hesitated. “Not yet.”

She paused, then nodded. “Email is fine.” She typed again. “Where are you staying?”

He repeated the address, slowly this time. She corrected the spelling once, asking him to say it again. He felt his face warm as he spoke, unsure of his pronunciation.

“All right,” she said finally. “You can go. Keep this paper.”

“Thank you,” he said, his voice quieter than he intended.

He stepped away from the counter, standing for a moment with the paper folded awkwardly in his hand. He was not entirely sure if he had done it right. He walked toward the seating area and sat down, holding his backpack close to his feet.

Minutes passed. Then more minutes. He watched people come and go. Some hugged family members. Some argued quietly. Others laughed, relieved to be home. He felt separate from all of it, as if he was observing through glass.

After a while, his phone buzzed. An email. He opened it slowly. It confirmed the claim. No promise. Just information.

He stood again and returned to the counter. A different staff member was there now, a man with glasses.

"Excuse me," Aaryan said. "My bag."

The man glanced at the paper. "Claim number?"

He handed it over.

The man typed. "Not yet. You can wait."

"How long?" Aaryan asked.

The man shrugged. "Hard to say."

So Aaryan waited. He shifted seats. He drank water from a fountain. He watched the baggage belt start and stop. Each time it moved, his heart lifted slightly, then settled again when nothing appeared.

Finally, after what felt like hours, a woman wheeled a small cart through a side door. On it were a few lonely suitcases. Aaryan stood without thinking, stepping closer.

She read out numbers. One by one, people stepped forward.

Then she paused. "Black bag. Red strap."

His chest tightened. "Yes," he said, stepping closer. "That's mine."

She checked the tag. Compared it to his paper. Then nodded. “Here you go.”

He reached out and took the handle. The bag felt heavier than he remembered, but solid. Real.

“Thank you,” he said, this time with certainty.

As he walked away, pulling the suitcase behind him, he felt a quiet relief settle in his body. It was not joy. It was not celebration. Just the simple comfort of having one familiar thing in a place where everything else was new.

Outside, the doors slid open with a hiss, and the city announced itself all at once.

“Taxi?”

“Bus pass?”

“Hey, you need a ride?”

Cars surged past, horns sharp and constant. A train rattled overhead. The air smelled of fuel and fried food and something sweet he could not place. He stopped near the curb, turning in a slow circle, unsure which sound to follow first.

A vendor waved at him. “You want a hot dog? Very good.”

He opened his mouth, then closed it again. “No, thank you,” he said carefully.

The vendor smiled and kept calling out to the next passerby, his words tumbling quickly, confidently. Aaryan watched people move through the space with ease, laughing, arguing, and gesturing freely. He adjusted his bag again, shifted his weight from one foot to the other, and swallowed.

For a moment, he felt oddly transparent, like he was standing inside the scene rather than part of it. He took a breath, then another, forcing himself to step forward into the crowd.

He asked a man waiting at a bus stop, holding up his phone. "Excuse me," he said carefully. "This place… how to go?"

The man leaned in, squinted at the screen, then spoke rapidly, pointing down the road and then back the other way. Aaryan caught only fragments. Left. No, right. Two blocks. Bus maybe. He nodded, thanking him, though he was no clearer than before.

As he dragged his suitcase along the uneven pavement, a memory surfaced without warning. His mother standing near the doorway back home, reminding him to call as soon as he arrived. His father explaining, in calm detail, what to do if he felt lost.

"Ask people," he had said. "Someone will help."

At home, directions were simple. Streets had stories. Every corner had a reference point. Here, everything looked the same, and nothing felt anchored.

It took hours. Missed turns. A bus ride he boarded too late and exited too early. By the time he finally reached the building, his arms ached, and his patience was worn thin. He stood outside for a moment, checking the address again, then looking up at the faded numbers bolted above the door. This was it.

The residence was smaller than he had imagined. The stairs were narrow and uneven, the railing loose under his hand. Each step creaked as he climbed. The hallway was dim, lit by a single flickering bulb. The smell of cooked lentils and detergent hung in the air. He walked slowly, dragging his suitcase behind him, until he reached the door at the end.

It took two knocks before it opened.

“Aaryan?” his cousin said, relief crossing his face.

“Yes,” Aaryan replied, forcing a smile.

“Come in. You look exhausted.”

The door stuck before opening fully, just as he had been warned. Inside, the room was bare. A bed pushed against the wall. A small table with two mismatched chairs. Clothes folded neatly in one corner. A single window looked out onto a brick wall so close it felt like it was part of the room itself.

“Sorry,” his cousin said, stepping aside. “This is all I could manage.”

“It’s fine,” Aaryan said quickly. “It’s more than enough.”

His cousin took the suitcase from his hand. “Put it here. Sit. You must be hungry.”

Aaryan sat on the edge of the bed, his body finally giving in. The silence felt heavy, broken only by the hum of traffic outside.

“You made it late,” his cousin said, opening a small container. “Flight issues?”

“Bag was lost,” Aaryan said. “Found it after a long time.”

His cousin nodded. “It happens.”

They ate quietly for a few minutes. The food was simple but warm.

“You can stay here for now,” his cousin said carefully. “But only for some time.”

Aaryan looked up. “I understand.”

“I came only six months ago,” his cousin continued. “I’m still figuring things out. Rent is high. Space is small.”

“It’s okay,” Aaryan said. “I’ll find something.”

They sat back, the tiredness easing just enough for conversation.

"You need work soon," his cousin said. "Anything to start."

"Yes," Aaryan replied. "Anything."

"There is someone," his cousin said after a pause. "Ravi. He's been here much longer. Knows people. Can get you some factory work. Or maybe warehouse."

Aaryan nodded. "That would help."

"I'll call him tomorrow," his cousin said. "For now, rest."

His cousin turned off the light. Moonlight streamed in through the broken, drapeless window, allowing just enough visibility to make out the shape of the room.

Aaryan lay back on the bed later, staring at the ceiling. The room was quiet. Temporary. He could feel it. Still, for tonight, it was shelter. As he closed his eyes, he held onto one thought. This was only the beginning.

That night, he lay awake on the unfamiliar mattress, the city humming faintly outside. At home, nights were full of sound. Dishes clinking. Someone coughing in the next room. A television murmuring in the background. Here, silence felt sharp. He stared at the ceiling and wondered when, exactly, excitement had turned into something heavier.

Days slipped into weeks, and by then he had moved into a small, pen-like room of his own, narrow and quiet, with no income to support himself. The silence often pulled his thoughts back to his father's voice, firm and unyielding, reminding him not to overstay anyone's welcome. Leave quickly, even if there is no work yet. Use the money we gave you. Ask for more if you must.

Those words stayed with him as he lay awake at night, staring at the low ceiling. He understood what his father meant. Pride mattered. So did standing on your own feet. But unemployment weighed heavily on him. Each passing day without work felt like a slow drain on the savings his family had gathered for him with years of sacrifice. He imagined the quiet calculations back home, the careful budgeting, the trust placed in him. The thought made his chest tighten.

He wanted to move forward, not backward. He wanted his struggle to be his own, not something his family had to carry from afar. Yet without work, every expense felt louder, every meal more deliberate. He balanced his father's insistence on self-reliance against the fear of becoming a burden, trapped between urgency and uncertainty, waiting for the moment when effort would finally turn into opportunity.

Whatever excitement of the foreign land remained began to thin. Aaryan woke each morning to the same unfamiliar ceiling and the same muted street sounds beyond his window. He checked his phone often, scrolling through old messages and photos, lingering longer than necessary before locking the screen again. Each attempt at conversation felt like a small test he was never quite prepared for.

One afternoon, his phone buzzed while he sat on the edge of the bed, shoes still on from a walk that had led nowhere. He glanced at the screen. Ravi. He straightened instinctively and answered at once.

"Hello?" Aaryan said.

"You free right now?" Ravi asked. His voice was steady, practical.

"Yes," Aaryan replied. "Always."

Ravi let out a short breath. "There's a warehouse hiring. Night shift. Packing and loading. Not easy work, but it's work. I can put your name in."

Aaryan did not hesitate. "I'll take it."

There was a brief pause on the other end. “You sure? Hours are long. Pay is basic.”

“I’m sure,” Aaryan said. His voice came out firmer than he felt. “Anything is fine.”

“All right,” Ravi said. “Be ready tonight. I’ll text you the address and what to bring.”

“Thank you,” Aaryan said quickly, the words tumbling over each other. “Thank you so much.”

When the call ended, the room felt different. Nothing had changed. The walls were the same. The window still looked out onto the same stretch of street. But his chest felt lighter. He sat there for a moment, phone in his hand, then stood up and began to prepare, moving with a quiet urgency, as if stopping might give doubt the chance to catch up.

The next day, his day stretched out in small, uncertain steps. He folded his clothes carefully, then unfolded them again, unsure what would be right for a warehouse job he had never seen. He checked the address Ravi had sent, copying it into a notebook as if writing it down would make it more real. Outside, he paced the narrow sidewalk, counting the hours until evening, rehearsing simple introductions in his head. Every so often, he stopped and reminded himself that work, any work, was a beginning.

Hunger crept in quietly. He ignored it at first, telling himself he would eat later, after things felt more settled. But the empty feeling in his stomach grew harder to dismiss. He walked past a row of small restaurants, their windows fogged with heat and smell, unsure where to go in. Each doorway felt like another test, another place where words would be expected of him. He stood there for a moment, hands in his pockets, then pushed one door open and stepped inside.

For Aaryan, ordering food became an exercise in hesitation too. That evening, he stood at the counter of a small restaurant, menu held in both hands, eyes moving slowly from top to bottom. The words refused to settle. Burrito. Taco. Bowl. He mouthed them quietly, trying to make sense of sounds that carried no memory.

"What can I get for you?" the cashier asked, fingers already hovering over the screen.

He froze. "Uh," he said, then cleared his throat. "This one." He pointed to a picture filled with color and careful arrangement, trusting the image to speak in his place.

"Chicken or beef?"

He hesitated, then nodded. "Yes."

The cashier paused, then smiled faintly and completed the order. When the food arrived, the smell was rich and inviting. He took a cautious bite, then another. The flavors were strong and unfamiliar, enjoyable in their own way. Still, something was missing. He ate slowly, aware of the empty chair across from him. It tasted good, but it did not taste like home. That realization settled quietly, heavier than he expected.

He left the restaurant as the sky began to darken, the streetlights flickering on one by one. The address Ravi had sent led him to the edge of an industrial area, where long buildings stretched low and wide, their windows glowing harsh white. Inside the warehouse, the air was cold and smelled of cardboard and dust. A supervisor handed him a vest and spoke quickly, pointing down rows of shelves stacked higher than he could see. Aaryan nodded more than he understood, watching the movements of others and copying them the best he could.

The work was physical and repetitive. Lift. Scan. Stack. Push. His arms burned within the first hour, and his back protested with every bend.

Instructions came fast, sometimes shouted from across the floor. When he missed a word, he followed the rhythm instead, matching his pace to the people beside him. No one asked questions. No one lingered. The machines hummed constantly, filling the space between thoughts.

By the time his shift ended, his legs felt unsteady. He stepped outside into the cool night, breath rising in short clouds, and checked his phone just to confirm the time. He had made it through. That was enough for one day.

The rest of the week moved in a blur. Sleep came in short stretches. Meals were quick and forgettable. Each night, he returned to the same building, the same rows, the same motions. His body adjusted slowly, learning where to brace and when to rest. The fear of doing something wrong softened into quiet focus. He learned which supervisor spoke slower, which coworker nodded instead of talking, which corners of the warehouse stayed warmer.

By the end of the week, his hands were rough, his shoulders sore, but there was a small, steady satisfaction in knowing where he needed to be and what was expected of him. The job did not offer comfort or pride, but it gave structure. It gave him somewhere to go. And for now, that was enough to keep him moving forward.

On most evenings, he walked without a destination. The streets were crowded, alive with voices and movement. Families passed him in clusters, children racing ahead while parents called after them. Groups of friends leaned into one another, laughing easily, sharing jokes that needed no explanation. He slowed his pace, pretending to check his phone while listening to the rise and fall of their conversations.

At a nearby park, he sat on a bench and watched. An elderly couple shared a snack, tearing pieces and passing them back and forth. Teenagers argued playfully, their hands moving as much as their voices. He smiled at the familiarity of it all, even though none of it belonged to him. The laughter reached him and then moved on, leaving him behind in the same quiet space he carried everywhere.

Back in his small room, the silence pressed in. He tried to cook, following recipes on his phone, but the dishes never turned out quite right. He missed the smell of spices warming in oil, the sound of someone calling his name from another room, the comfort of shared meals where words were not required.

The conflict grew slowly, almost politely. He recognized parts of himself that felt unchanged, his values intact, his sense of right and wrong steady. Yet everything around him seemed to ask for adaptation. He learned when to speak, when to pause, and when silence was safer. Some days, the future felt close, something he could almost reach. Other days, nostalgia arrived without warning, tightening its grip until it was hard to breathe.

One evening, he stood by the window, looking out at the brick wall across from him. The glass reflected his face faintly, layered over the city beyond. He studied that reflection and wondered which version of himself he was becoming. The one shaped by memory, or the one shaped by necessity. Perhaps both, he thought. Perhaps identity was not something preserved, but something carried forward, altered by each place it passed through.

He understood then that belonging was not immediate. It was not granted upon arrival. It was built slowly, through discomfort, through failure, through persistence. He was not lost, exactly. He was in transition.

With that thought, he stepped back from the window. Tomorrow would come. And with it, another chance to learn how to exist in the space between where he came from and where he was going.

However, things weren't that straightforward from thereon either. It was the small acts that hurt the most. One morning at a coffee shop near his apartment, the barista looked up and said, "Hi, how are you today?" Her tone was light, automatic. Aaryan froze, his mouth opening a second too late.

By the time he managed a quiet, "Good," she was already turning away, calling out another order.

He stood there with his wallet half open, heat rising to his face, replaying the pause again and again as if it had been louder than it truly was.

Another afternoon, he accepted an invitation from a coworker to join a casual gathering at a shared apartment. People sat cross-legged on the floor, laughing, passing snacks, talking over one another with ease. Someone told a joke, and the room erupted. Aaryan smiled when everyone else did, though he had not understood the punchline. When someone asked him where he was from, he answered, but the conversation moved on before he could add more. He spent the rest of the evening holding a paper cup, nodding at the right moments, counting how often he checked the time.

But he continued the pursuit to connect until he finally got his break. One evening, he sat alone on a bench outside a grocery store, bags at his feet. His shoulders were tight, his back curved inward. He noticed how often he held his breath without realizing it. That was when the thought surfaced, uncomfortable but clear. He was not only afraid of misunderstanding others. He was afraid of being misunderstood. Fear had been deciding for him when to speak, when to stop, when to disappear.

The next day, at a pedestrian crossing, an older man standing beside him glanced over and said, "Cold today, isn't it?"

Aaryan hesitated, then nodded. "Yes. Very."

The man smiled, satisfied, and said nothing more. The light changed. They crossed in silence. It was a small exchange, barely an interaction, yet it stayed with Aaryan longer than most conversations had. He had answered. He had not retreated.

At a neighborhood market later that week, he returned to a fruit stall he had passed many times. He pointed to apples, then held up two fingers. The vendor asked something he did not understand. Aaryan shrugged apologetically.

The vendor laughed, picked two apples anyway, and said, "Good choice."

When Aaryan said thank you, the words came out clearer than he expected.

In these moments, small and imperfect, Aaryan felt parts of himself return. He learned that discomfort did not mean rejection. It meant learning. Language did not always require fluency. Sometimes it only required presence. Each interaction, no matter how brief, taught him something about patience, about timing, about allowing silence to exist without shame.

CHAPTER THREE

# Isolation and Reflection

By most measures, Aaryan was doing well.

He had learned the routes of the city without relying on maps. He knew which subway car stopped closest to the stairs, which coffee shop moved fastest during the morning rush, and which streets to avoid after dark. At work, people greeted him by name now. Some asked about his weekend. Others waved as he passed. He had even started staying back occasionally, joining casual conversations that drifted from work into life.

From the outside, his days looked full.

He spoke more confidently than he had during his first weeks. His English no longer felt fragile in his mouth. He understood jokes, even made a few of his own. There were lunches eaten with coworkers and short exchanges with neighbors in the hallway. He was learning how things worked here, how people moved, how time felt faster and looser all at once.

And yet, somewhere beneath that progress, something else was growing quietly.

He noticed it most in crowded places. Standing in line at a grocery store, surrounded by people talking into phones or scanning shelves with purpose, he felt oddly suspended. Everyone seemed to know where they were going, what they were reaching for. He followed the same routines, picked the same items, and paid without trouble. Still, the sense of belonging did not follow. It was as if he had learned the steps of a dance without ever feeling the music.

At work, conversations flowed easily now, but they often stopped just short of where he lived. His coworkers spoke about childhood memories, high school rivalries, and family jokes passed down for years. He listened, smiled, and nodded at the right moments. He was included, but lightly, like someone invited into a room without being handed a chair. No one meant to exclude him. They simply did not know how to place him yet.

Even laughter sometimes made him aware of the distance. When a group laughed loudly at lunch, he joined in, then felt a familiar pause inside himself. Not sadness exactly, but a faint dislocation. The sound reminded him of home, of voices overlapping around a table, of laughter that needed no explanation. Here, the laughter was warm, but it did not carry his history.

He began to understand that loneliness did not always arrive as silence. Sometimes it came wrapped in noise and motion.

On weekends, he explored the city. He visited public parks where families gathered, children running between benches while parents watched with tired affection. He sat nearby, scrolling through his phone, occasionally exchanging smiles with strangers. Once, a man asked him to take a photo of his family. Aaryan agreed, framed the shot carefully, handed the phone back, and received a grateful thank you. The interaction lasted less than a minute, yet it stayed with him longer than expected. A brief crossing of lives, then separation.

At night, video calls home became both comfort and weight. His mother asked if he was eating well, if he was warm enough, and if people were kind. He answered honestly, but selectively. He spoke about work, about the city, about how much he was learning. He did not mention how often he felt like a guest in his own life.

One night, after a late shift, he sat on the edge of his bed and called home. The screen flickered before settling on his mother's face, softly lit by the single bulb in the room behind her. She adjusted the phone, moving too close at first, then pulling it back.

"Can you see me?" she asked.

"Yes, Ma," Aaryan said. "I can see you."

She studied his face for a moment, her eyes narrowing slightly. "You look thinner."

He smiled, a small practiced smile. "It's the camera."

"Don't joke," she said, though her lips curved despite herself. "Are you eating properly?"

"Yes. I eat," he said. "There's food everywhere here."

"What kind of food?" she asked at once. "Hot food? Or just bread and outside things?"

"Hot food," he replied quickly. "Rice sometimes. Vegetables. It's fine."

She nodded, unconvinced. "And work? You started, no?"

"Yes," he said. "Warehouse work. Night shift."

Her eyebrows lifted. "Night?"

"Only for now," he added, sensing the worry rising. "It's okay. I manage."

She was quiet for a second, then asked, "People are treating you well?"

"Yes," he said. "They're fine. Everyone is busy."

"Busy is okay," she said softly. "Busy means no one has time to trouble you."

He glanced down at his hands, then back at the screen. "How is Baba?"

She turned the phone slightly, calling out, "He's asking about you."

A voice came from off-screen. "Tell him not to skip meals," his father said.

"I'm not skipping," Aaryan said, a little louder. "I'm fine."

His mother looked at him again, her gaze lingering. "If it gets too hard, you tell us," she said. "Don't carry everything alone."

He nodded. "I know."

"And money?" she asked, carefully. "You have enough for now?"

"Yes," he said. "I'm managing."

She reached out toward the screen, her hand hovering as if she could touch his face through it. "Take care of yourself," she said. "We pray every day."

"I know," he said. "I miss you."

"We miss you too," she replied. "Work hard. Rest when you can."

The call ended after a few more words, the screen going dark in his hand. He sat there for a long moment, the room suddenly quieter than before, the weight of everything he had not said settling in around him.

He thought often about how easy belonging had once been. At home, it was not something he questioned. It was built into the air, into shared language, shared memory, shared silence. Here, belonging felt conditional, something to be earned slowly through consistency and time. He wondered if that was simply adulthood or if it was the cost of crossing borders.

Walking home one evening, he passed a row of restaurants glowing with light and conversation. Through the windows, he saw people leaning toward one another, hands moving as they spoke. He kept walking, hands in his pockets, aware that he could step inside any one of those places. The doors were open. Still, he hesitated.

That was when he understood the contradiction he was living inside. His world was expanding, yet something within him felt unanchored. He was becoming capable, functional, even confident, while another part of him quietly searched for familiarity, for recognition that went deeper than names and routines.

Perhaps, he thought, this was not failure but transition. A space between who he had been and who he was becoming. Growth, he realized, was not always loud or visible. Sometimes it was lonely. Sometimes it required standing in the middle of connection and admitting that connection alone was not the same as belonging.

But there were moments that offered brief sparks of belonging. At a community cultural festival, he had met Leila. She approached him with an easy laugh, pointing at a handmade decoration and asking, "Have you tried this yet?" He shook his head, unsure of the words to respond, but she didn't seem to notice. Instead, she handed him a small piece, and as he tasted it, the sweetness and spice spoke louder than his faltering English ever could. He laughed along with her, and in that laughter, he felt a glimmer of belonging. For the first time, he realized that communication didn't only happen with words; it was in shared smiles, gestures, and the willingness to meet halfway.

Despite these moments, a gnawing unease persisted. He thought of the friends he had left behind, the effortless conversations that had required no translation or explanation. He remembered the quiet evenings at home, when the simple act of sitting at the dinner table with family filled him with warmth. Here, he had meals alone, sometimes calling home just to hear his mother's voice, to bridge a distance that no phone could truly close. Even as he shared laughter with new acquaintances, a part of him measured each interaction against the deep, unspoken histories of his past.

What troubled him the most was the cultural contradictions that greeted Aaryan at every turn. On one hand, he marveled at the efficiency of the city:

clean streets, organized transport, the sheer convenience of goods and services within arm's reach. On the other hand, he felt disoriented by the casual detachment between people. In his homeland, neighbors greeted one another across fences, children played together until sunset, and the rhythm of daily life carried an unspoken, shared heartbeat. Here, the closeness he expected was replaced by polite distance. People exchanged nods or small smiles, but conversations rarely lingered. Doorways remained closed, and yards felt like barriers instead of spaces for community. The absence of collective warmth unsettled him, as though life was operating at a pace too fast to accommodate shared humanity.

Sports and pop culture offered another layer of dissonance. The baseball fields and basketball courts that drew enthusiastic crowds were thrilling to watch on television, but he struggled to join in the rituals. His love for cricket was rarely replicated amongst the locals. The chants, the cheers, the inside jokes about players he had never heard of, each was a subtle reminder that he existed outside the current. While teenagers streamed past on skateboards or rollerblades, headphones clamped over ears, immersed in music he did not know, he felt both intrigued and excluded. Even the humor in movies and sitcoms seemed laced with references that eluded him, leaving him to laugh half-heartedly at punchlines he only partly understood. The ease with which Americans navigated their own cultural landscape felt like a skill he had yet to acquire, a language of living that was not only spoken but performed.

Daily interactions intensified the sense of individualism he could not quite reconcile. Aaryan noticed how neighbors carefully managed their distance: lawns manicured with precision, conversations often truncated, and personal schedules guarded like sacred rituals. In his homeland, a cup of sugar lent over a fence could ignite friendships; here, borrowing even a teaspoon would require explanation, and the offer was sometimes politely refused. The lack of shared responsibility or spontaneous gatherings left him uneasy. There were no group outings, no block parties, no collective rhythms of life, only parallel existences that sometimes intersected in brief, polite encounters.

Even within workplaces and classrooms, the contradictions persisted. Hierarchies were subtle, but individual opinions carried weight; collaboration existed, but often at the expense of connection. The emphasis on personal achievement clashed with the communal approach he had internalized, making even small team projects feel like a performance where fitting in required negotiation of unspoken codes. At times, he caught himself longing for the cacophony of overlapping lives, the unpredictability of collective laughter, and the comfort of knowing someone would notice his absence or his small successes without prompting.

This constant negotiation of norms, expectations, and behaviors was exhausting. He found himself observing patterns, taking mental notes, trying to align gestures, speech, and timing with an invisible map of cultural cues. Yet, with every step forward, the awareness of difference lingered. Even in moments of connection, like sharing a coffee with a colleague who smiled warmly, Aaryan sensed the undercurrent of individuality; the emphasis on self, the prioritization of personal space, the subtle distance that could never be bridged completely. He needed to make peace with it.

It was a paradox that both intrigued and frustrated him. The society offered freedom and opportunity, but it demanded self-reliance in ways that sometimes felt isolating. He admired the efficiency and the order, yet mourned the absent embrace of shared life.

CHAPTER FOUR

# The First Step Forward

Aaryan surprised himself with how quickly he learned the surface of the city. Within weeks, he knew which bus arrived late, which grocery store had the cheapest vegetables, and which streets felt safer after dark. He learned the rhythm of traffic lights and the quiet rules of standing in line. He figured out how to order coffee without holding up the queue and how to smile at strangers without expecting a conversation to follow. From the outside, it looked like an adjustment.

Every morning, he stepped into the city with a little more confidence. He walked past familiar storefronts, nodded at the same security guard outside the subway station, and recognized faces without knowing names. The city no longer felt hostile. It felt neutral. But neutrality carried its own weight. He could function, yet he could not fully participate. The barrier was always there, invisible but firm. Language stood between him and ease.

Simple tasks demanded effort. At the pharmacy, he rehearsed sentences in his head while waiting in line, only to forget them when the cashier spoke too quickly. At the bank, he nodded along to explanations he only half understood, signing papers with a tight chest and quiet fear. Once, at a grocery store, the cashier asked him a casual question about his day. He froze, smiled awkwardly, and answered with a single word that ended the exchange too soon. As he walked out, bags cutting into his palms, he replayed the moment again and again, imagining what he could have said if the words had come to him in time.

Crowded places made the gap more obvious. On buses filled with chatter, he sat silently, listening to conversations blur into sound rather than meaning. At work, colleagues joked during lunch breaks, their laughter quick and unforced. He laughed when they laughed, though he often missed the reason. No one was unkind. They invited him, included him, smiled at him. Still, he felt like he was watching life through glass. Present, but not fully inside.

At cafés, he noticed how easily people spoke to baristas, how names were remembered, preferences recalled. He envied the ease more than the connection itself. Once, he mispronounced a word while ordering, and the barista corrected him gently. The interaction lasted seconds, but the heat rose to his face and stayed long after he sat down. He did not feel angry or embarrassed. He felt tired. Tired of measuring every word, tired of feeling younger than his age, smaller than his thoughts.

At night, he reflected on how far he had come and how far he still felt from himself. He was not failing, but he was not moving forward either. He realized that familiarity without voice was a fragile thing. Without language, even confidence felt borrowed. He could survive like this, he knew. Many people did. But survival was not why he had come.

The turning point did not arrive as a dramatic moment. It came quietly, during an ordinary afternoon. He was sitting in a public library, surrounded by people reading, typing, and studying. He noticed a small bulletin board near the entrance, cluttered with flyers. One caught his eye. A community language class. Free. Open to all. He stood there longer than necessary, reading the details again and again, as if the paper might disappear if he looked away.

Doubt followed him home. He thought about the frustration of learning, the mistakes, the exhaustion of starting from the beginning. He thought about how many times he had already felt small. But another thought pushed through, steady and clear. Nothing would change if he stayed silent. The city would continue to move around him, and he would remain on its edges.

That night, he filled out the registration form online. His finger hovered over the submit button longer than it should have. Then he clicked.

For the first time in months, the decision felt like his own.

Not perfect. Not fearless. But intentional.

The approval email arrived three days later. It was brief and polite, with a start date, a room number, and a time written in plain language. Aaryan read it more than once, letting the words settle. He told himself it was just a class. One hour. Nothing more. Still, when the day came, his body did not treat it lightly.

He arrived early and stood across the street from the community center, watching people go in and out. Some walked with purpose, others lingered on the steps, laughing, talking, moving easily. He checked the address again, even though he knew it was right. His palms were damp. His chest felt tight in a familiar way, the way it always did when he was about to speak in a place where words mattered.

Inside, the hallway smelled faintly of coffee and cleaning spray. Voices echoed from different rooms. He followed the signs until he reached the classroom door. It was open. Chairs were filling up. A whiteboard stood at the front with neat writing already on it. He stayed where he was, just outside the frame of the room, close enough to hear, far enough to escape if he needed to.

He told himself to step in. He did not move.

Students continued to arrive, greeting each other softly, some confidently, others with the same careful politeness he recognized in himself. The room grew fuller. He shifted his weight from one foot to the other, his mind racing through reasons to leave. He could come back another day. He could practice alone. He could do this later, when he felt ready.

The door opened wider.

A woman stepped out, shorter than he expected, with silver hair pulled back neatly and a cardigan draped over her shoulders. She carried herself with ease, the kind that comes from long familiarity with people and places. She looked around the hallway, then noticed him.

She smiled.

"Are you here for the class?" she asked.

Her voice was gentle, unhurried. No pressure in it.

He hesitated, then nodded.

"Good," she said, as if that settled everything. "Come. We were waiting for you."

She placed a light hand on his arm, not pulling, not pushing. Just guiding. The touch surprised him. It was warm. Familiar in a way he had not felt in a long time. Before he could think too much, he found himself inside the room, seated in an empty chair near the middle.

"I am Fatima," she said, once everyone was settled. "And this is our space. You do not need to be perfect here."

She said it plainly, like a fact.

The class began slowly. Introductions were optional. Participation was encouraged, not demanded. Fatima spoke clearly, repeating herself when needed, never rushing anyone. When someone struggled, she waited. When someone made a mistake, she smiled and moved on without drawing attention to it.

Aaryan kept his eyes on his notebook, copying down words carefully. His hand shook at first, then steadied. Around him, others stumbled through sentences, laughed at themselves, tried again. The sound of imperfect language filled the room, and for the first time, it did not feel like a weakness. It felt shared.

Halfway through the class, he noticed a familiar face across the room.

Leila.

She caught his eye and smiled, her expression bright with recognition. She lifted her hand in a small wave, then tapped the notebook in front of her, as if to say, *You made it.*

She was volunteering, helping newer students, whispering clarifications, passing out papers. When she leaned over to him, she spoke softly.

"I am glad you came," she said.

So was he, though he did not say it out loud.

When Fatima asked for volunteers to read a short sentence, the room fell quiet. Aaryan's heart beat faster. He did not raise his hand. Neither did he look away. Fatima's gaze landed on him, not sharp, not expectant.

"Would you like to try?" she asked. "Only if you want."

He swallowed and nodded.

The words came out uneven, broken in places. He paused. He corrected himself. No one interrupted. No one rushed him. When he finished, Fatima nodded once.

"Good," she said. "You spoke."

That was all.

When the class ended, people lingered. Chairs scraped softly against the floor. Conversations continued in half sentences, gestures filling the gaps. Fatima stood by the door, thanking everyone as they left. When Aaryan reached her, she smiled again.

"Same time next week," she said. "You belong here."

Outside, the air felt different. Lighter.

He did not suddenly feel fluent. He did not feel fearless. But something had shifted. He had stepped inside. He had stayed.

As he walked home, he realized that the hardest part had not been learning the language.

It had been believing he was allowed to try.

Three months passed without Aaryan noticing their weight. The classes became part of his week, as ordinary and steady as the walk to the bus stop or the morning coffee he no longer hesitated to order. What once felt like a single act of courage slowly turned into routine, and routine into growth.

By the end of the third month, he was no longer seated in the middle of the room, silent and careful. He spoke more. Not perfectly, but willingly. He asked questions. He laughed when he misspoke. When the results were posted on the notice board, his name appeared under the next level. He read it twice to be sure.

Promoted.

The word stayed with him all day.

What surprised him more was what followed. Fatima asked if he would consider volunteering for the beginner class, just a few hours a week. Helping with worksheets. Sitting beside newcomers who looked the way he once had, shoulders tight, eyes cautious, hands hovering above blank pages.

"You know how it feels," she said simply. "That matters."

On his first day as a volunteer, he stood near the door, watching new students arrive. Some clutched folders tightly. Some avoided eye contact. One man lingered in the hallway, unsure whether to step inside. Without thinking, Aaryan walked over.

"Are you here for the class?" he asked, the words steady, natural.

The man nodded.

"Come," Aaryan said. "It is okay."

Only later did he realize what had happened. He sat alone that evening, the room quiet except for the low hum of traffic outside, and replayed the moment in his mind. There had been no effort, no rehearsal, no fear of choosing the wrong words. He had simply stepped forward. The memory unsettled him in a gentle way. Not long ago, he had been the one hovering at the door, measuring whether he belonged, waiting for permission to enter. Now, without noticing the shift, he had become a steady presence for someone else. It did not feel grand or heroic. It felt ordinary. And that was what stayed with him. Growth, he understood, had not arrived as a single turning point but through quiet repetitions of courage. Somewhere between learning, failing, and trying again, he had crossed a line he once could not see. He was no longer just surviving the space he occupied. He was shaping it.

The change reached beyond the classroom. His days moved differently now. He spoke to the cashier without rehearsing. He asked coworkers about their weekends. He made small jokes that landed more often than they fell flat. Conversations still required effort, but they no longer felt like obstacles to survive. They were bridges.

At the café where he once pointed at pictures, he now ordered with ease, even correcting himself when he misspoke. At the bus stop, he exchanged greetings with the same elderly man each morning. These moments were small, but together they reshaped his sense of place. He was no longer just passing through his days. He was part of them.

The biggest shift, though, happened quietly. One afternoon, Fatima asked him if he would be willing to help with curriculum support for the incoming group. Simple writing tasks. Short explanations. Articles meant to ease newcomers into the language and the system.

"In English," she added, watching him carefully.

He hesitated, then agreed.

The first article took him hours. He revised every sentence. He read it aloud, listening for rhythm, clarity, and honesty. When it was published in the center's newsletter, his name appeared beneath the title. Not as a student. Not as a learner.

As a contributor.

Later, he received a small badge from the center, pinned to his bag. "Article Writer and Curriculum Assistant." He smiled when he saw it, not because of the title, but because of what it represented. Proof that effort compounded. Proof that fear did not have the final word.

On his walk home that evening, he slowed his pace. The city moved around him as it always had, busy, loud, indifferent. But he no longer felt invisible within it. He thought about the version of himself who had stood outside that classroom door, convinced he did not belong inside.

All it had taken was one step.

Not confidence. Not certainty. Just movement.

He understood now that courage did not arrive fully formed. It grew in fragments, shaped by repetition and patience. By showing up even when doubt was louder than hope. By accepting help. By offering it back.

His life had not transformed overnight. It had shifted gradually, almost quietly. But the direction had changed, and that made all the difference.

Aaryan knew there would be more challenges ahead. New words to learn. New spaces to enter. New versions of himself to meet. But he carried something solid now. The knowledge that daring to begin, even clumsily, could alter the course of a life.

And that was an achievement no language barrier could take away.

CHAPTER FIVE

# Cultural Clashes

Aaryan arrived at Ravi's modest apartment with a mixture of anticipation and tension. The aroma of fresh pizza and a hint of beer from a plethora of opened cans greeted him at the door. The room was filled with colleagues and friends, laughter bouncing off the walls, yet he immediately felt the familiar tug of uncertainty. Here, everyone seemed at ease, gestures flowed naturally, conversations intertwined with references he sometimes did not understand, jokes punctuated with cultural shorthand he could only partially grasp.

Ravi noticed him hovering near the entrance. "Aaryan, come in! Don't just stand there," he said warmly, gesturing toward a chair beside the small dining table. "You've got to try the shawarma. Leila helped me make them."

Aaryan nodded, adjusting his bag, his palms slightly sweaty. He had been practicing how to participate, how to laugh without overthinking, how to respond without shrinking. Yet, the fear of saying the wrong thing kept him rooted for a moment.

Leila, who was leaning against the counter, arranging plates, caught his hesitation and smiled.

Taking a deep breath, Aaryan moved closer, holding a plate. He watched the others chatter, noticing the small cultural cues he had begun to recognize, the rhythm of informal conversation, the way interruptions weren't impolite but participatory, the nods and laughter that punctuated ideas rather than words themselves.

When Ravi brought up the city's annual sports festival, Aaryan's anxiety rushed back. In the past couple of weeks, football had become a topic that came up at every gathering, and he had no clue what to say. He fell back on his usual answer. "I don't follow football much," he admitted, trying to sound casual.

Sam laughed, clapping him lightly on the shoulder. "That's okay! You can watch. You'll learn. But you know, it's not just the game, it's the banter, the energy. It's how we… connect."

Aaryan nodded, trying to absorb it, then seized a chance to share his own culture. "In India, cricket is… everyone talks about cricket. Even kids," he said, smiling nervously. "We play in the streets. Sometimes neighbors join in, even if they don't know you. It's… loud, chaotic, fun."

Leila's eyes lit up. "That sounds amazing! I wish our streets were like that here."

Encouraged by the reaction, Aaryan continued. "And food and spices. Everyone knows the smell of your neighbor's cooking. You smell it in the morning and evening. You eat together, even if you didn't plan it."

Sam leaned back, intrigued. "That sense of community… I see what you mean. Here, it's quieter. People respect privacy, but it can feel… distant if you're not used to it."

Aaryan felt a flicker of connection. Finally, someone recognized the depth behind what he was trying to explain. "Yes. Sometimes I… miss that," he admitted, his voice quieter. "It's beautiful, but it can be lonely here. I want to share, but I am… careful. Not to… overwhelm?"

"You don't overwhelm," Leila said softly. "You add to it. Perspective, stories, food… that's the point of gatherings like this."

Gradually, Aaryan started noticing the small openings in the room, the way a laugh could invite him in, the way a question about his family encouraged a story rather than judgment, the way Ravi made room in conversations for him to speak, genuinely listen, and be understood. Each exchange required effort, each sentence a little risk, but the reward was subtle and profound.

By the end of the evening, he realized that understanding American culture did not mean erasing his own. The sports references, the casual jokes, the tendency to keep personal life compartmentalized, they were patterns to learn, not chains to wear. And sharing his own habits, tastes, and memories from home was not a disruption; it was a bridge.

As he walked home that night, Aaryan thought about the evening, replaying his friends' excited faces and the small spark of curiosity that his stories had ignited. He understood, perhaps for the first time, that belonging was not about blending completely. It was about being present, about letting others see him in fragments and stories, and learning to navigate both worlds without losing either.

The idea stayed with him for days before he said it out loud.

Days later, as Aaryan stood at his kitchen counter, stirring onions into hot oil, the familiar crackle filling the small apartment, a passing thought filled his mind. The smell, cumin, ginger, garlic, rose quickly, dense and comforting. It reminded him of Sundays at home, of the television already on in the background, of voices arguing over field placements and batting orders long before the toss.

*India versus Pakistan is next week,* he thought. *What if I organize a game night with some Indian food?*

The memory carried warmth, but also hesitation.

The faces from Ravi's dinner party surfaced in his mind, familiar now, but still edged with formality. Ravi himself, generous and observant. Leila, curious and warm, always asking questions that went beyond politeness. A few others, including Sam, whose names he still sometimes rehearsed before speaking them aloud. They had listened to him that night. They had asked about food, about cricket, about where he came from. Not in a way that reduced him, but in a way that made room.

Still, the doubt came quickly.

*What if they don't like the food?*

*What if they don't understand the match?*

*What if it becomes awkward, too loud, too foreign?*

He wiped his hands on a towel and looked around the apartment. It was small, plainly furnished. No dining table big enough for many people. No couch that didn't sag slightly in the middle. It did not look like a place meant for gathering.

But Aaryan was determined. He knew that doing is way better than thinking. Without wasting another moment, he called Ravi.

The line clicked. "Hi. Want to join for a cricket match and some Indian food coming Sunday?" Aaryan said, as if rehearsed but polite.

“I didn't even realize cricket season was still on,” Ravi said, smiling. “Or does it never really end?”

Aaryan laughed softly. “For us? It never ends.”

Ravi spoke again. “India versus Pakistan is a big deal, right? You mentioned it once.”

“Yes,” he said. “Very big.”

“Bigger than a Super Bowl?” Ravi asked curiously.

Aaryan hesitated, then replied. “For me. Yes.” Aaryan's tone carried the confidence he had struggled to find.

There was a pause. The kind that opens a door or closes it.

"Yeah, sure, buddy. We were planning another meetup this Sunday, I think none of us will have any problems coming to your house for some cricket and delicious Indian food."

Aaryan's heart began to thud.

"Okay, see you all," he replied and put the phone down nervously.

On the match day, he woke early, nerves buzzing beneath the excitement. He went to three different stores to find the right spices, rejecting substitutes that didn't feel quite right. He called his mother once, asking casually about a dish he already knew how to make, just to hear her voice confirm it.

"Don't overthink," she said. "Food knows when it's made with fear."

He smiled at that.

By the time people arrived, the apartment smelled alive. The television was set up, cushions dragged onto the floor. A pot of biryani rested on the stove. Bowls of chutney and sliced onions crowded the counter.

Ravi was first to arrive, carrying a six-pack.

"I hope beer is acceptable," he said.

Aaryan laughed. "Today, everything is acceptable."

Leila came next, holding a bag of chips. "I Googled cricket rules," she admitted. "Still confused."

"You'll learn by watching," Aaryan said. "Or by shouting. Both work."

As more people filtered in, the space filled quickly—with voices, with questions, with the easy chaos of shoes kicked off and jackets draped over chairs.

"What's this called?" Sam asked, pointing to the biryani.

"Biryani," Aaryan said. "Rice, spices, meat. It's not a side dish. It's the event."

They chuckled.

When the match began, the room quieted. Aaryan explained the basics, runs, wickets, and overs, pausing when someone interrupted with a question.

"So they don't just keep hitting forever?" Ravi asked.

"No," Aaryan said, smiling. "Eventually, everyone falls."

At one point, India lost an early wicket. Aaryan groaned instinctively, hands on his head.

Leila glanced at him. "Is it bad?"

"It's… emotional," he said.

As the game unfolded, so did the evening. People went back for seconds. Someone asked about the rivalry, not just the sport, but the history. Aaryan answered carefully, honestly, without simplifying or hardening the edges.

"We cheer," he said. "But there is also pain. Pride. Things we inherited, whether we wanted to or not."

Ravi nodded slowly. "I appreciate how you explain it. Not like a lecture. Like a story."

Later, during a tense moment near the end of the match, the room held its breath together. When India won, Aaryan let out a shout he hadn't known he was holding back. The room erupted, not because everyone understood the significance, but because they understood *him*.

Ravi clapped him on the shoulder. "This," he said, gesturing around the room, "this is what you meant at the dinner. Coexistence."

Aaryan looked around. Empty plates, tired smiles, people still asking for one last explanation, one last taste.

"Yes," he said quietly. "This is it."

When everyone finally left, the apartment felt larger, not emptier. The silence was gentle.

He began washing dishes slowly, replaying the evening in his mind, not the perfect moments, but the real ones. The questions. The misunderstandings. The laughter that bridged them.

The water ran warm over his hands as he scrubbed a plate someone had asked about twice, curious about the spices, unsure of the name. He remembered pausing, then answering without searching for the right version of himself. He had not simplified. He had not adjusted his words to fit what he thought others might understand. He had spoken as he was, and they had leaned in to listen. That stayed with him.

He thought about how often he had learned to shrink himself. How many times he had rehearsed sentences in his head, weighing accents and reactions before speaking. That night, none of that had happened. The food had carried its own language. The stories had unfolded naturally, uneven and honest. Some guests had asked clumsy questions. Some had made wrong assumptions. But no one had turned away. They stayed. They tasted. They listened.

He set another dish on the rack and realized something had shifted without his noticing. He had not been translating his culture into something safer or easier. He had not been explaining himself in advance. He had simply been present. That presence had been enough. It had invited curiosity instead of judgment. It had allowed space for mistakes without discomfort.

What surprised him most was the subtle pride that followed. Not the kind that demanded recognition, but the steady satisfaction of knowing he had shared something real. He thought of the recipes learned at home, the habits absorbed without question, the customs that once felt ordinary and now carried weight. Sharing them did not feel like a performance. It felt like continuity. Like carrying something forward without losing it.

He dried his hands and leaned against the counter, letting the silence settle. The evening had not erased differences. It had placed them side by side. That felt right. He understood then that coexistence was not about blending until nothing stood out. It was about allowing things to exist fully, without apology.

For the first time, he realized he had not been translating himself. He had simply been present. He loved sharing his culture with others and was glad he did such a great job.

CHAPTER SIX

# Finding Community

After the party, the feeling did not leave him. It stayed in small ways, lingering long after the last dish had been washed and the echoes of laughter had faded from his apartment. He found himself replaying moments from the evening while walking to work, while waiting for the bus, while standing in line for coffee. The questions people had asked him. The curiosity in their voices. The way the room had shifted once stories were shared, once food had been passed around, once the cricket match had stopped being just noise on a screen and turned into something communal. It struck him that so many of them had known him for months, yet had only just begun to see where he came from.

With that realization came an unfamiliar restlessness. He began to sense that his culture was not something meant to be quietly carried or selectively revealed. It was meant to be shared. Not as an explanation or a defense, but as an offering. He wanted people to know more than surface-level facts or borrowed stereotypes. He wanted them to understand the warmth and contradictions, the humor and the grief, the pride and the unease. At the same time, he felt a pull toward those like him, the ones who stood between places, carrying both happiness and loss in equal measure. He wanted to speak to them too, to say that the confusion was real, that the loneliness was not imagined, and that the joy, when it came, was worth naming.

He tried, at first, to talk about it out loud. With Ravi. With Leila. With a few classmates after language sessions. The words always reached his mouth and then hesitated there, crowded by doubt. He worried about sounding self-important. He worried about not being clear enough. Most of all, he worried about being misunderstood. Conversations drifted elsewhere, as they often did, and he found himself nodding along while something inside him remained unresolved. He knew he wanted to say more. He just did not yet know how, or where, or to whom.

It was during one of those quiet, uncertain moments, when the urge to speak was strong, but the courage was still forming, that his attention shifted toward another possibility. He found a newspaper lying at the edge of the coffee table at the cafe, creased and slightly yellowed from other hands. Aaryan had not been looking for it. He had only meant to skim headlines while waiting for his coffee to cool. But the title caught him—*Between Two Homes: A Cambodian Life in America.*

He read the first paragraph. Then the second. By the third, he was submerged.

The writer described arriving in the United States as a child, the smell of fish paste clinging to clothes, the embarrassment of opening lunchboxes at school, the slow erosion of language at home, and the quiet grief of watching parents struggle in a country that demanded speed and certainty. The sentences were not grand, but they were precise. Honest. The kind of writing that did not try to impress, only to testify.

Aaryan felt something tighten in his chest.

He reread a line about identity not being lost, only layered. It echoed in him like a bell. For a moment, he forgot his coffee entirely. What stayed with him was not the cultural facts—the festivals, the food—but the intimacy. The courage to say: *This is how it felt.*

He folded the paper carefully and carried it with him the rest of the day, pulling it out again on the bus, then later at the community center. By evening, a thought he had been avoiding finally named itself.

*I have a story too.* And now he had a different kind of space. One that did not interrupt, did not rush, and did not demand perfection before allowing him to begin.

Yet, the idea unsettled him more than it excited him. Writing was one thing. He had always liked words, even when they betrayed him. But writing publicly, in English, for strangers? That felt reckless. He thought of his pauses, his grammar slipping when emotions rose, the way his tongue sometimes outran his confidence.

*How to get myself in this paper?* He asked himself.

The answer arrived quickly and cruelly: *With good enough English.*

That night, he opened a blank document on his laptop and stared at it until the screen dimmed. He typed a sentence, deleted it. Typed another, simpler one. Deleted that too. Everything sounded false or fragile. He imagined an editor's red pen, imagined readers judging not his ideas but his mistakes.

By the time he closed the laptop, the doubt had settled heavily. Wanting to be heard, he realized, was not the same as believing you deserved to speak.

Two days later, after class, he found Fatima organizing papers at her desk. The room smelled faintly of dry-erase markers and old books. He hesitated at the doorway, as he often had once before, then knocked lightly.

"Come in," she said, not looking up. "You look like someone carrying a question."

He smiled despite himself. "Is it that obvious?"

"To me? Always," she replied, finally meeting his eyes. "Sit."

He handed her the folded newspaper. "I read this," he said. "About a Cambodian immigrant. He writes about his life here."

Fatima skimmed the article quickly, nodding. “Yes. I remember this. It caused quite a response.”

“I couldn’t stop thinking about it,” Aaryan continued. “About how… he explained things. Small things. Like food. Language. Feeling invisible.” He paused. “I thought—maybe I could do something like this. Write about Indian culture here. About… life.”

Fatima leaned back, studying him carefully. “And?”

“And then I thought,” he said quietly, “who would publish me? My English is not… always strong. I don’t want pity. I don’t want people to read just because I am an immigrant. I want them to read because it means something.”

For a moment, she said nothing. Then she smiled, not indulgently, but with recognition.

“You’re asking the wrong first question,” she said. “You’re asking where you will be allowed to speak. You should ask how you will begin speaking at all.”

He frowned slightly. “What do you mean?”

“Newspapers are destinations,” Fatima said. “Not starting points. You don’t wait for permission to have a voice.”

Aaryan shifted in his chair. “But how? I don’t know editors. I don’t even know if people would care.”

“People care about honesty,” she replied. “And consistency. Not perfection.” She tapped the newspaper. “This writer didn’t start here. He wrote before anyone noticed. Probably badly at first.”

That landed gently, but firmly.

She continued, “Start a blog.”

"A blog?" The word sounded almost naïve to him.

"Yes," she said. "Your space. Your pace. Write about what you know: your mornings, your food, your confusion at grocery stores, your memories of home. Write about what you miss, and what surprises you."

He hesitated. "And the language?"

"We work on it," she said simply. "I can help. Editing. Proofreading. But the voice must be yours. I won't polish away your thinking."

That evening, Aaryan chose a simple platform. No elaborate design, no grand title. He named it after a phrase his mother often used when describing resilience—**Between Spices and Silence**. The words felt right, though their meaning was still settling in his mind. They were both intimate and universal, carrying the memory of home and the quiet space he had carved for himself here. Sitting in his small room, he stared at the blank page on the screen. The cursor blinked steadily, and for a long moment, it seemed to demand that he begin, though he was unsure how.

He picked up his notebook, the one he carried everywhere, frayed at the edges, pages filled with scribbles, reminders, and phrases he had overheard in the new city. He flipped to a blank page and began to write by hand first. The pencil felt different from typing, slower, more deliberate, and somehow more honest. Each word required thought. He paused often, rereading the line, erasing, and rewriting. The first attempt was awkward, almost stiff, the sentences too rigid. He crumpled the page and started again, reminding himself that he was not writing for anyone else yet. He was writing to see his thoughts clearly, to hold them outside himself.

He began with the small things, the details that filled his days and carried his memory of home. Standing in an American grocery store aisle, staring at twenty different kinds of milk, he had felt a pang of nostalgia. At home, the corner shop had always offered just a few choices, the familiarity comforting. He typed the words slowly, hesitant at first, unsure if they would make sense to someone who had not lived the same life. He described the colors of the labels, the smell of fresh bread in the bakery section, the quiet hum of fluorescent lights overhead. He lingered on the feeling of being overwhelmed, not in fear, but in awe of how different life could be when every small action demanded conscious thought.

Next, he wrote about the festivals. Diwali had always been loud, bright, and relentless in his hometown, with streets spilling over with decorations, laughter, and the smell of sweets. Here, celebrations were smaller, private, subdued. Families gathered indoors. The sound of crackers was replaced by the hum of television channels airing the same scenes. He struggled with how to explain the ache of missing that sensory fullness without exaggerating, without making it sound like mere complaining. He paused, scrolled back over what he had written, and deleted a line, then another, until only what felt necessary remained.

The hardest part was translating feelings into words. He typed a paragraph about learning when to smile at strangers and when to keep his gaze low. In India, a nod or a small greeting could spark a conversation that lasted hours. Here, people were polite but distant. He wanted to show the subtle difference, the skill of reading people, the constant mental adjustment. He wrote and rewrote sentences, trying to convey that this was not about judgment but about learning a new rhythm. Each time he thought he had found the right phrasing, he read it aloud and found it sounded stiff. He tried again, letting the words fall naturally, even if the grammar was not perfect.

Aaryan also reflected on the quiet moments. The small apartment, the sounds of his neighbors, the way morning sunlight fell across the window sill. He realized he had been absorbing these details without naming them, but now he could give them life on the page. He described the hum of the street outside his window, the smell of coffee from the café below, the distant laughter of children. Each observation demanded attention, patience, and clarity. He found that writing required slowing down in a way that thinking alone did not. Every moment became significant, every sensation an entry point into the story he was building.

He wrestled with structure. Should he start chronologically, from the moment he arrived, or should he begin with the present, with reflections? He tried one approach, only to delete paragraphs and begin again. Hours passed. He became aware of the small sounds in the room: the low buzz of the heater, the tapping of keys, the occasional creak of the old floorboards. He realized he had to accept imperfections, that the first draft was never final, that writing itself was part of the journey he was describing.

Aaryan paused, stretched, and sipped from a mug of tea he had left cooling beside him. He watched the steam rise and vanish, noticing how even a small comfort could anchor him. Then he returned to the screen and began typing again. He added little scenes: the cashier at the corner store who mispronounced his name but smiled, the bus ride that always made him nervous because he did not know the stops, the first time he had felt confident ordering a meal alone. These were fragments of life, small but vivid, and they carried truth. He learned that honesty did not always need to be dramatic. It could exist in the simple recounting of moments lived fully.

The act of writing became almost meditative. He realized he was not just telling a story; he was creating a space where he could reconcile the old and the new. Sometimes he stopped mid-sentence, staring at the page, unsure how to continue. He would close his eyes, breathe, and imagine the scenes as if reliving them. Slowly, words returned, guided by memory and emotion. He found joy in discovering how the language he had learned could carry nuance, even when imperfect, even when sentences bent slightly under his uncertainty.

He also struggled with self-doubt. He would read a paragraph and question whether it made sense, whether it was too small, too mundane. He compared himself silently to other writers he had seen online, wondered if his voice mattered, if anyone would understand. Then he reminded himself that this space was first for him. He wrote because he wanted to remember, to process, to honor the experiences he had lived. The page was patient. The cursor waited. No one judged him here.

After a staggering nine hours, the first draft was complete. He leaned back, hands resting on the keyboard, and looked at the words. The post was long, rambling at times, but it captured the texture of his life: the strangeness of grocery aisles, the quiet of festivals, the small victories in language, the stillness of his room at night. Then came revision. Two more hours passed as he rearranged sentences, trimmed repetitions, simplified awkward phrasing, and highlighted the details that made him feel most alive. He read it aloud multiple times, hearing the cadence, adjusting words that felt flat. He realized that writing required both patience and courage, the courage to expose simple truths that were often overlooked.

Finally, he paused. He scrolled to the top and reread the post from beginning to end. The sentences were simple, but they carried the weight of observation. The post reflected his voice, his perspective, and his presence in this new world. He saved it with a soft exhale, feeling both nervous and satisfied. He knew it would not reach a wide audience immediately. Perhaps no one would read it. Perhaps someone would. That did not matter yet. What mattered was that he had named his experience, held it in his hands, and given it shape in the world.

Sitting back, he realized that the act of writing had been a quiet revelation. He understood that he could translate his life without losing its essence. He could capture what it meant to be here, balancing memory and adaptation, without over-explaining or performing. Between Spices and Silence was not just a title. It was a lens, a way to observe, to reflect, and to share. And for the first time since arriving in this new land, he felt he had begun to tell his story in a way that was entirely his own.

Before publishing, he sent the draft to Fatima.

Her feedback was careful. "This sentence is strong," she wrote. "Here, simplify. Don't explain too much, trust the reader." She corrected grammar, yes, but more importantly, she asked questions. *What did you feel here? What did you choose not to say out loud?*

When he finally clicked "publish," his heart raced as if he had stepped onto a stage.

The first week, only a handful of people read it. One comment came from a woman who wrote, "I'm not Indian, but this reminded me of my father." Another student said, "I feel this every day and didn't know how to say it."

That was enough.

He kept writing. About cricket matches watched alone on a laptop. About teaching coworkers how to pronounce his name—and learning to insist they try. About phone calls home that grew shorter, not because love faded, but because lives diverged. He wrote about pride and guilt coexisting, about how assimilation often asked for silence in exchange for safety.

Each post sharpened his English not through the rules of textbooks or grammar exercises but through use. Writing became a conversation he held first with himself, then with the invisible audience who might read it. Words, once heavy and awkward, began to feel like tools in his hands. A sentence was not just a collection of letters but a way to carry thought clearly from his mind onto the page. If a line felt off, he would rewrite it. If a paragraph seemed crowded or confusing, he would take it apart, spread the pieces on the screen, and rebuild it. Every revision forced him to examine his thinking, to notice when he was vague or unclear, and to push himself toward precision.

At first, the process was slow. He would spend an hour on one paragraph, rearranging words, searching for the right rhythm, the right sound. Sometimes he grew frustrated and left the page for a while, staring out the window at the street below. The rhythm of life there—the footsteps, the bus engines, the occasional laughter—became part of his awareness, part of his understanding of pace, tone, and flow. Gradually, he realized that writing regularly was not about perfection but about presence. Each post carried pieces of his day, his thoughts, and his reflections. Each post became a small mirror showing how far he had come, how much he could see and articulate about the world around him.

The responses were modest, but they were meaningful. He began to notice that people did not read to critique him, not really; they read to recognize themselves. And that recognition, that quiet resonance, gave him confidence he had not anticipated. He felt a sense of connection that was subtle but strong, a reminder that though he was far from home, he was not entirely alone.

Months passed. Each post required the same care, the same attention, the same quiet patience. He began to plan topics more deliberately. A simple observation of a street corner could unfold into a reflection on human behavior, on adaptation, on memory. He wrote about the way light fell on the brick walls at dusk, how a cup of chai felt different in his small apartment compared to his family kitchen, about the routine of daily life and how it revealed habits he had never noticed before. He wrote in the morning when his mind was fresh, sometimes late at night when the city had quieted, when the air felt still enough to hear his own thoughts. Each time, he typed slowly, rereading, adjusting, learning not just English but the rhythm of expressing himself fully.

Then, one quiet Sunday morning, months after he had begun writing, Aaryan opened his laptop as usual. He had a mug of tea beside him, steam curling in the early sunlight that filtered through the thin curtains. His notebook lay open on the desk, notes for the next post scattered across the page. He expected another ordinary morning of writing and revising, maybe posting, maybe waiting for someone to read. But the screen loaded slowly, and when it did, he froze.

There it was. Staring back at him in stark black and white: **1,000,000 views.**

The number felt unreal. He blinked. Then he refreshed the page once. Then again. The number did not change. One million. He had imagined success, yes, but not like this. Not in a moment so quiet. It was too large, too sudden, too precise. He sat back in his chair, hands resting lightly on the keyboard, and just looked.

For a long while, he did not move. He listened to the hum of the refrigerator in the next room, the faint squeal of tires on the street outside his window. He could hear the clatter of dishes from the apartment above, the occasional bark of a dog, the distant call of a vendor from hours ago. Life continued as it had before. The world did not pause for this number, but something inside him shifted. The feeling he expected—loud, explosive, triumphant—did not come. Instead, it was soft and heavy, a weight settling quietly into place. It felt like acknowledgment, like validation not from applause or accolades, but from the simple, steady rhythm of people noticing, understanding, and connecting.

He scrolled through the comments. They were small, simple, honest. Someone had written: *"I didn't know someone else felt the same way in the grocery aisle."* Another said: *"Your words reminded me of home, and now I can feel it here."* Others thanked him for writing plainly, for sharing the ordinary moments that somehow felt extraordinary when placed on a page. He read comment after comment, and with each one, he realized that the achievement was not the number. The number was just evidence. What mattered was the impact, the quiet recognition that his observations, his thoughts, his life, resonated with someone else.

Aaryan leaned back and let himself remember how he had started. The first post had taken him three hours to write, another two to revise. He had agonized over every word, every detail. The sentences had been clumsy, full of pauses and half-formed ideas. He had doubted if anyone would care. Yet here he was, months later, realizing that the effort, the patience, and the persistence had created a bridge. A bridge built from careful observation, from slow reflection, from honesty about his life in a place that was new, strange, and sometimes lonely.

He thought of the people he had written about—the cashier, the bus driver, the neighbors, the quiet festivals, the grocery aisles—and understood that they had always been part of the story, whether they knew it or not. He thought of the evenings spent revising a paragraph again and again, wondering if it sounded natural, and realized that each repetition had strengthened his voice. Every hesitation, every correction, every pause had contributed to a clarity he had once thought impossible. He could see it now, in the patterns of his writing, in the way words finally carried thought without stumbling, in the way strangers on the other side of a screen could understand him.

For the first time, he felt that writing was not about perfection or immediate recognition. It was about presence. About noticing. About observing life so carefully that it could be offered to someone else without distortion. The views, the number, the comments—they were secondary. The primary achievement was that he had learned to carry his mind fully, and to share it without fear.

Aaryan closed the comments section and let himself sit quietly. He could still hear the city outside his window, distant and indifferent, moving along without pause. He could hear his own breathing. He could feel the chair beneath him and the cool morning light on his hands. And for the first time in months, maybe in years, he felt a sense of stillness that was both rare and deep. The number was startling, but what struck him more was the realization that he had arrived in a space where his thoughts, his experiences, his voice, could matter.

He thought of his family, of Ravi, of Leila, of the small lessons he had learned about language, culture, and patience. He thought of the way writing had forced him to slow down, to notice details he would have overlooked, to give meaning to ordinary moments. And he understood that this milestone, quiet though it appeared, was a reflection not of sudden luck, but of months of deliberate effort, reflection, and care.

Aaryan reopened the post, this time not to check numbers but to read the words themselves. He traced the sentences with his eyes, absorbing the texture of what he had written. He saw how much he had grown, not just as a writer, but as someone capable of noticing, reflecting, and communicating a life that straddled two worlds. For the first time, he felt that writing was no longer a challenge. It was a tool. A companion. A lens. It had given him a way to exist fully in this new country while carrying home in his mind and heart.

The achievement, then, was not the views. It was the clarity. The connection. The steady, quiet knowledge that through observation, patience, and persistence, he could translate a life fully lived into words that others could understand. And in that, he felt the softest, most enduring victory of all.

Emails began to arrive from places he had never been. A nurse in Texas wrote about working double shifts and being asked daily where she was "really from." A student in Michigan shared how he had stopped speaking his mother tongue altogether, afraid it would hold him back. A man from Kenya, living in California, wrote about the shame he felt when he sent money home but still struggled to pay his own rent.

They never met. They never shared a room. But they began to speak to each other in the comment sections, replying not just to Aaryan, but to one another. Advice was exchanged. Frustrations were named. Jokes appeared, dry and familiar. Slowly, the blog stopped feeling like his alone.

With encouragement from Fatima, he started experimenting. One afternoon, standing at a bus stop under gray skies, he took a photo of his worn notebook resting on his knee, the edges curled from use. He posted it with a short caption about how ideas often came when he was waiting, when life forced him to pause. The response was immediate. People shared their own photos. Coffee cups. Bus tickets. Work badges. Each image carried a small confession.

Realizing that he now has a voice, his posts became sharper. Not angry, but clear. He wrote about the systems that made daily life harder than it needed to be. Immigration paperwork was written in a language even native speakers struggled to understand. Job interviews where accents mattered more than ability. Housing forms that asked for histories that newcomers could not provide. He questioned why resilience was expected, but support was optional.

When three of his posts crossed a million views, the local news website reached out. The email sat unread for a full day because he was convinced it had been sent to the wrong person. When he finally replied, his hands shook. The article they published focused on immigrant voices finding space online, and his blog was at the center of it. His photo appeared beside the headline. He barely recognized himself in it.

The attention changed things, but not in the way he feared. It did not make him louder. It made him more careful.

He began fact-checking his reflections, linking resources, and inviting guest writers to contribute. A Syrian architect wrote about being asked to “start over” despite decades of experience. A second-generation immigrant challenged Aaryan’s perspective, writing about guilt from the other side. He published it without hesitation. The comments that followed were thoughtful, difficult, and necessary.

In his daily life, the blog gave him an unexpected steadiness. Conversations felt easier. When someone asked where he was from, he answered without rehearsing. At cafés, he took photos without embarrassment. He wrote captions that did not explain themselves. He trusted readers to meet him halfway.

Late one night, scrolling through messages, he realized something that startled him. The fear that once followed every sentence he spoke had loosened its grip. Not disappeared, but softened. Writing had not fixed everything. It had given shape to what once felt formless.

Before shutting down his laptop, he typed a short note at the end of his latest post.

"This space began as a way for me to understand myself. It has become a place where we understand each other."

He did not polish it. He did not second-guess it.

He clicked publish and closed the lid, carrying with him the quiet knowledge that connection, once imagined as something distant and fragile, had grown real through words, shared truth, and the courage to speak before feeling ready.

CHAPTER SEVEN

# The Turning Point

The email arrived on a Tuesday morning, tucked between routine updates and meeting reminders. Aaryan almost ignored it. The subject line was vague enough to suggest nothing urgent, but something made him pause. He opened it while his coffee cooled beside him, one hand still resting on the edge of the desk.

"Due to recent restructuring…"

He read the first line twice. Then a third time.

The words blurred after that. Budget constraints. Role redundancy. Effective immediately.

He sat back in his chair and stared at the screen, waiting for the feeling to catch up. It did not arrive all at once. Instead, there was a hollow quiet, like the moment after a door shuts and the sound has not yet settled. He refreshed his inbox, half expecting another message that would explain this away. None came.

A knock sounded on the desk divider. "You got a minute?" his supervisor asked, already stepping closer.

Aaryan nodded, though his mouth felt dry.

They sat in a small conference room. His supervisor spoke carefully, choosing words that sounded practiced. "This is not about performance," he said. "You have done solid work. The company is cutting back. Entire teams are being affected."

Aaryan listened, nodding at the right moments. He heard himself say, “I understand,” though he was not sure he did. When it was over, he shook hands, collected a few personal items from his desk, and walked out with a cardboard box that felt too light for what it represented.

Outside, the day moved on without him. Cars passed. People laughed on the sidewalk. He stood there for a moment, unsure where to go, then started walking home because it was the only decision that felt possible.

That evening, he sat on his bed with his phone in his hands, staring at his mother’s name on the screen. He had not missed a transfer in months. Every paycheck, a portion went home. It paid for groceries, electricity, and medicine. It was not just money. It was reassurance.

He called anyway.

“Hello?” his mother answered, cheerful as always.

“How are you?” he asked.

“Fine, fine. Your father was asking about you this morning. Did you eat?”

He closed his eyes. “Maa,” he said softly. “I need to tell you something.”

There was a pause. “What is it?”

“I lost my job today.”

The silence on the other end stretched longer this time. “Lost?” she repeated. “How?”

“They downsized. It was sudden.”

“And your next payment?” she asked, not accusing, just practical.

“I… I will manage something. Maybe not this month. But I will figure it out.”

She exhaled slowly. “Beta, don’t panic. We will adjust. Your father has some savings. You focus on finding work.”

“I am sorry,” he said, the words catching in his throat. “I promised—”

“Enough,” she interrupted gently. “You did not fail us. These things happen.”

Aaryan ended the call and set the phone down carefully on the edge of his bed. The familiar hum of the room seemed louder now, every sound sharper, each creak of the floorboard amplified. He sat for a long time, letting his back sink into the mattress, staring at the bare wall across from him. Nothing had changed in the room, yet it felt heavier. His mother’s voice, calm and measured, still echoed softly in his mind. He wanted to believe her reassurance, wanted to feel it, but the knot in his stomach refused to loosen.

The money he sent home had been a lifeline, a tether to the life he had left behind, a proof that his family’s investment in him was not wasted. Each paycheck was more than currency; it was a reassurance, a silent message that he could survive here and provide for them even from afar. Without it, that proof felt fragile, slipping through his fingers. The thought of disappointing them gnawed quietly, relentlessly. He had promised. He had committed. And now, for the first time, he had failed to keep that promise.

He tried to trace the day in his mind, the last hours at the office. He had arrived as usual, greeting colleagues he had come to know, exchanging the small jokes and polite smiles that marked routine. Then the meeting. The words. Downsizing. Immediate. Surprising. The cardboard box, empty but heavy with meaning. He remembered the awkward silence in the room, the careful avoidance of eyes, the murmured goodbyes that felt too light. Outside, the city carried on, indifferent. Cars honked. People laughed. The sun moved across the sky. Life did not pause.

He let his hands fall onto his lap, folded together, and thought of his father. The stern yet gentle voice that had always pushed him to act, to plan, to be independent. His father had warned him about overstaying, about leaning too much on family support. He had sent him here with the expectation that Aaryan would move quickly, find work, and make something of himself. That expectation had felt heavy before, and now it pressed down with sharper weight. How could he fail so soon, after months of careful planning, careful saving, careful living?

Aaryan's eyes drifted to the window. The street outside looked familiar yet distant, the buildings lined in the gray light of evening. He thought of the paths he had walked to get here, the bus rides, the early mornings, the evenings spent revising resumes, making calls, trying to learn not only language but the rhythm of this new place. None of it seemed enough. The thought of his family, trusting him with their savings, trusting him to create a future, brought an ache he could not voice.

He began to run through possibilities, practical and immediate. Could he find work tonight? Impossible. Tomorrow? Perhaps, but the hours would be long, the pay uncertain, the fit unclear. And yet, he could not wait. He had to move. He had to act. Every delay felt like letting the gap widen between himself and the responsibility he carried. But at the same time, he felt the weight of uncertainty pressing down. Every option seemed fragile, every path risky.

Aaryan closed his eyes and let his thoughts drift backward and forward at once. He remembered the warehouse job, the first small steps he had taken when he arrived. How hesitant he had been, how awkward, how unsure of every word, every gesture. And yet he had done it. He had worked, learned, grown, made mistakes and corrected them. He remembered the encouragement from Ravi, the late-night talks about navigating the city, about surviving, about persistence. Could that connection help now? Could he reach out again and find a new way forward?

The thought of calling Ravi, of asking for guidance, felt both necessary and humbling. It reminded him that independence did not mean isolation, that asking for help was not weakness. But even as he considered it, a quiet voice in his mind reminded him of the stakes. He had sent money for months, carefully, for groceries, for bills, for his parents' peace of mind. If he asked for help too often, would he appear weak? Would they see him as incapable? The questions twisted quietly, leaving him more restless than before.

His gaze wandered across the room again. The bare walls, the thin mattress, the small table. This was his life now, his responsibility, his world to shape. And yet, the world outside seemed daunting, distant, unfamiliar in ways he had once embraced but now felt overwhelming. Every shadow in the room felt longer, every sound amplified, every silence louder. He realized that he was alone here, truly alone, in a way he had never been before. Family was far. Friends were few. The city was indifferent. And the choices rested entirely with him.

Aaryan rose slowly and moved to the window. He leaned his forehead against the cool glass, watching the lights flicker across the street. People moved about, some rushing home, some walking slowly, some laughing. The city continued. It was not waiting for him, and yet he was part of it, whether ready or not. He drew a long breath, deep enough to fill the quiet corners of his chest. He could feel the tension loosen, very slightly, as if the act of breathing itself reminded him he was alive, he was capable. He had faced harder days than this before, days when language, culture, and unfamiliarity seemed insurmountable. And yet he had survived.

Sitting back down, he opened his laptop. The cursor blinked patiently, waiting for action. He could write emails, send resumes, call contacts. He could make a plan, piece by piece, step by step. The practicalities mattered more than the panic, more than the shame, more than the worry that had lingered since the call ended. He realized that worrying would solve nothing. Action, thought, and persistence would carry him forward.

And still, the quiet ache remained. It was not something he could ignore or push away. It was the weight of responsibility, the reminder that his family had entrusted him with more than money—they had entrusted him with their faith, their hope. He thought of his mother's words: *Beta, don't panic.* They were simple, measured, reassuring, but they also held expectation. He would not panic. He would act. He would find a way.

He opened a notebook beside him and began writing. Not resumes. Not applications. Not plans. He wrote about the day, about the feelings, about the knot in his chest that refused to disappear. Writing was always a way to untangle the jumble in his mind, to see clearly what needed attention. He wrote about responsibility, about failure, about hope, about the quiet hum of the apartment and the distant sounds of the city. Words came slowly, carefully, measured. Each sentence was deliberate, a bridge from despair to clarity.

As he wrote, he realized he had been thinking too much in extremes—failure or success, panic or calm. Life, he saw, was not about extremes. It was about persistence, about small steps, repeated over days and weeks. Each word in his notebook, each idea, each plan, was part of a foundation he was building. The loss of one job did not erase the months of work, learning, and growth. It was a challenge, yes, but not a dead end.

By the time the evening passed into night, Aaryan felt something he had not expected. The weight had not vanished, but it had shifted, moved from tightness in his chest to quiet determination. He would call Ravi. He would explore the contacts he had built. He would send emails and applications. He would move, carefully, deliberately, because he had no choice but to do so—and because he could. The responsibility he carried, the promises he had made, the faith of his family, were not burdens to crush him; they were guides, pointing toward the next step.

He closed the notebook and lay back on the bed, feeling the thin mattress beneath him. The room was still the same. The city outside still moved without pause. But inside him, something had shifted. He was no longer just a boy far from home, afraid of failing. He was someone capable of acting despite fear, of thinking despite uncertainty, of moving forward despite loss. The first day of the rest of this chapter awaited him, and for the first time that evening, he felt ready to meet it.

The next few days blurred together. He updated his resume, rewrote cover letters, applied to positions that felt slightly out of reach and others that felt beneath his experience but safer. Rejection emails arrived quickly. Some did not arrive at all.

At the grocery store, he paused longer than usual, calculating prices in his head. Back home, he skipped meals without fully realizing it. Hunger was easier to manage than anxiety.

He met Ravi for coffee on Friday.

“You look tired,” Ravi said, studying him over the rim of his cup.

“I was laid off,” Aaryan said.

Ravi leaned back. “I am sorry. That is rough.”

“I don’t know how long I can stay afloat,” Aaryan admitted. “Rent. Bills. And sending money home.”

“You will find something,” Ravi said.

“That confidence,” Aaryan replied quietly, “feels borrowed.”

Ravi nodded. “Then borrow it for now.”

The language center became his anchor. He volunteered more hours, partly to feel useful, partly to avoid sitting alone with his thoughts. Fatima noticed immediately.

"You are quieter," she said one afternoon, handing him a stack of worksheets.

"I lost my job," he told her.

She did not rush to respond. She set the papers down. "Sit," she said.

They took two chairs by the window. "This country," she said, "is very good at making people feel disposable. Especially immigrants."

He gave a small smile. "That helps. A little."

"You are not your job," she continued. "But I know it feels like it right now."

He nodded. "I feel like I am failing everyone at once."

"Then let us break that thought," she said. "Who did you fail today?"

He thought about it. "No one. Not yet."

"Exactly," she said. "Focus on today."

At night, he struggled to sleep. His mind replayed old promises, imagined worst outcomes, and questioned choices he could not undo. He thought about the version of himself who had arrived here, hopeful and unsure, and wondered if that hope had been naive.

One afternoon, he received a message from Leila.

"Ravi told me. Are you okay?"

"Not really," he replied. "But I am trying."

They met at a park nearby. He told her everything. The job. The money. The fear.

She listened without interrupting. "You know," she said eventually, "losing my first job here felt like losing the ground beneath me. But it also pushed me to rethink what I wanted."

"I don't have the luxury of rethinking," he said. "People depend on me."

"They do," she agreed. "But they also want you standing, not breaking."

That night, he opened his laptop and stared at his blog dashboard. He had not written in weeks. Slowly, he began typing. Not about success. Not about lessons. Just about losses. About the shame of unemployment. About the quiet panic of not being able to send money home.

When he hit publish, he felt exposed. But also lighter.

The setback did not resolve itself quickly. There was no sudden offer, no neat conclusion. But something shifted. He stopped seeing the job loss as a verdict and started seeing it as a pause. Painful. Unwanted. Still survivable.

For the first time since the email, he slept through the night.

A week passed without work, and the quiet began to feel louder than the city outside his window. At first, Aaryan had told himself it was only temporary, a brief pause before things returned to normal. But by the seventh morning, the pause had turned into something heavier. He woke without urgency, no inbox to check, no place to be. That absence unsettled him more than exhaustion ever had.

He made tea and sat at the small table near the window. The cup warmed his hands, but his thoughts stayed restless. Losing the job was no longer just a shock. It had become a mirror.

No matter how gently others framed it, the truth was difficult to ignore. When the company had to choose, they chose to let him go. It was not personal, he knew that. Still, it was real. He had not been valuable enough to keep.

The thought stung, but it did not paralyze him. Instead, it sharpened something inside him.

If value could be measured, then it could also be built.

That morning, he opened a notebook he had not used in months. On the first page, he wrote a simple question. What can I do better than yesterday?

He did not start with ambition. He started with honesty.

He listed the gaps he could no longer ignore. His professional English still faltered under pressure. His technical skills were dated. He relied too much on effort and not enough on strategy. Reading it all in his own handwriting felt uncomfortable, but also clarifying. The problem was no longer abstract. It was defined.

He set rules for himself that day. Simple ones. No drifting. No waiting for motivation. He would treat improvement like a job until he found one.

Each morning began the same way. He woke early, showered, and dressed as if he were going somewhere important. It helped his mind take the day seriously. He cleared a corner of his room and turned it into a workspace. Laptop. Notebook. A printed schedule taped to the wall.

The first focus was language. Not grammar drills alone, but use. He recorded himself speaking on his phone, answering interview questions out loud. When he listened back, he cringed at first. The pauses. The fillers. The moments where confidence collapsed into silence. Instead of stopping, he took notes. Slower pace. Clearer structure. Simpler words.

He read articles daily and rewrote them in his own words. Not to copy, but to understand rhythm. How ideas moved. How sentences breathed. He paid attention to clarity more than complexity. Being understood mattered more than sounding impressive.

In the afternoons, he shifted to skill building. He enrolled in online courses he had postponed for years, telling himself he was too busy before. Now, there were no excuses. He chose courses that aligned with where he wanted to go, not just where he had been. Practical skills. Tools that companies actually used. He followed tutorials carefully, then repeated the exercises without guidance until he could do them from memory.

Progress was uneven. Some days, things clicked easily. On others, frustration returned, heavy and familiar. When that happened, he walked. Around the block. Past the same trees and stores. Movement helped him reset. Quitting did not.

Evenings became a time for reflection. He wrote about what he learned that day, not as achievements but as observations. What felt difficult. What surprised him. Where he resisted change. Slowly, patterns emerged. He saw how often fear disguised itself as fatigue. How avoidance felt like rest but led nowhere.

Money remained tight. He tracked every expense carefully, cooking simple meals and cutting anything unnecessary. The discipline did not feel like punishment. It felt like respect for the reality he was in.

One night, while reviewing job descriptions, he noticed something shift. The listings no longer intimidated him the way they had before. Instead of focusing on what he lacked, he began matching requirements to skills he was actively building. The gap felt narrower. Still challenging, but no longer impossible.

He updated his resume again, this time with intention. Not inflated. Not defensive. Honest and forward-looking. He framed his experiences as evolving rather than finished. He wrote cover letters that spoke clearly about growth, not desperation.

Most importantly, he changed how he spoke to himself.

Losing the job had bruised his confidence, but it had also stripped away illusions. He no longer believed effort alone was enough. Value had to be visible. Measurable. Useful.

That realization did not make him bitter. It made him focused.

By the end of the week, nothing external had changed. He was still unemployed. Still uncertain. Still unable to send money home. But internally, something had shifted. He was no longer waiting to be chosen.

He was building someone worth choosing.

And for the first time since the layoff, that thought did not scare him. It steadied him.

With Ravi's help, Aaryan picked up a series of odd jobs over the next few months, work that was often tiring and far from stable but enough to keep him going and restore a sense of dignity. He worked early mornings and late evenings, learned to adapt quickly, and treated every task as a chance to sharpen his discipline rather than dwell on disappointment. Those months tested his patience, yet they also grounded him. When the job offer finally arrived, it was unexpected and almost unreal. The role paid significantly more than his previous position and recognized the very skills he had been working to build in silence. Holding the offer letter in his hands, Aaryan felt not triumph, but quiet relief, the kind that comes from knowing that persistence, even in unglamorous moments, can slowly reshape the course of a life.

The day he was paid, Aaryan sent double the amount he used to send back home and ended his payday with a long call back home.

CHAPTER EIGHT

# Embracing Identity

A year had passed since Aaryan first arrived in this new country. The once-overwhelming blur of cultural signs, unfamiliar faces, and confusing social rules had gradually started to make sense. He could walk down the street and recognize the rhythm of the city, the cues in conversations, and the subtle nods of acknowledgment between neighbors. Even the public holidays carried meaning beyond the surface. He understood not just the actions, but the intentions behind them, and he began to see himself as a participant rather than a visitor.

Thanksgiving approached, and this year, Aaryan wanted to do more than attend. He wanted to contribute. Ravi had suggested they host a small gathering at his apartment, something that could combine the traditional elements of the holiday with a touch of the cultural exchange they all valued. Sam had offered to help with organizing, and Leila, ever enthusiastic about sharing her artistic touch, volunteered to decorate. Aaryan felt a mixture of excitement and nervousness. He wanted everything to be perfect, to honor the tradition while showing the warmth of his own personality.

The preparations began a week in advance. Aaryan spent hours reading online guides about Thanksgiving dishes, comparing recipes, and making lists. He decided to make pumpkin pie, roasted vegetables, and a traditional turkey for the group. From his own kitchen, he experimented, tasting sauces, adjusting spices, and sometimes laughing at the moments when things went wrong. The first attempt at the pie crust collapsed, leaving him frustrated but determined. Leila, visiting one evening to help with decorations, had noticed him muttering to himself and offered a simple smile.

"You'll get it," she said, setting down a bowl of pre-chopped vegetables.

Her presence was grounding. Aaryan realized that what he was building was not just a meal, but an environment of inclusion, something that mirrored his own journey. He reflected on the contrast from the first year when he had felt like an observer in cafes, unsure of how to respond to greetings or laughter. This time, he was orchestrating part of the celebration, a position that carried both responsibility and pride.

On the day of the gathering, Ravi arrived early, carrying a bottle of wine and his usual calm confidence. Sam came with bags of side dishes, offering a grin and teasing comments about Aaryan's careful notes and lists. Leila showed up last, her arms full of streamers, candles, and small decorative pumpkins she had found at the local market.

Aaryan opened the door with a nervous smile, and Ravi immediately clapped him on the shoulder.

"You've done a lot," he said. "Now let's see if it all works together."

In the kitchen, the three of them moved fluidly, chopping, stirring, and laughing. Aaryan found himself explaining the significance of certain traditions, like the story behind the Thanksgiving turkey and the idea of expressing gratitude for the year's experiences. Sam listened attentively, asking questions, while Leila added creative touches, arranging vegetables in artistic patterns and suggesting ways to make the table look inviting.

When the first guests arrived, Aaryan felt a subtle thrill. He greeted them, guiding them toward seats, explaining the dishes, and watching as they dug in, complimenting the food and sharing their own stories. The conversation flowed easily, punctuated by laughter, teasing, and genuine curiosity. Even the football game playing quietly on the TV became a point of engagement. Aaryan had never followed American football before, but Sam patiently explained the rules, the strategies, and the excitement of the sport. He watched the plays, asking questions, occasionally laughing along with the others' reactions. The atmosphere was warm, familiar, and inclusive, a sharp contrast to the first year when even small gestures of friendliness had felt unreachable.

During a lull in the activity, Ravi leaned against the counter, watching Aaryan move from guest to guest.

"You've changed a lot in a year," he said. "You have learned to belong."

Aaryan nodded, letting the words sink in. He thought about the months spent writing his blog, the long nights volunteering, the awkward attempts at conversation that had slowly built into meaningful connections. Each experience had brought him here, to this point, where he could contribute, guide, and share. He realized that belonging was not a sudden event, but a series of small, deliberate steps.

Leila wandered over with a tray of pumpkin pie slices, balancing them carefully.

"Your hands are steady now," she teased.

Aaryan laughed, accepting the plate. "Practice makes permanent, they say," he replied. "I just hope permanent is good."

As the evening continued, the group settled in around the table. Stories were exchanged about childhood holidays, family traditions, and even moments of awkwardness from moving to a new place. Aaryan found himself sharing anecdotes from his own past, from India, and describing the cricket matches he watched with friends and the lively debates over India versus Pakistan games.

Later, when the football game ended, Sam turned to Aaryan.

"Next year, you should host a cricket game outside," he said, half-joking. "I have no idea how it works, but I'll learn."

Aaryan smiled, a warmth spreading through him. "Maybe I will," he said. "And I'll teach everyone the rules. You'll all get to play."

It was a moment of quiet triumph, not about victory in a sport, but about the feeling of being understood, included, and valued. He reflected on the journey it had taken: the first hesitant steps into the community center, the moments of awkwardness and fear, and the gradual accumulation of trust and confidence. This Thanksgiving, he realized, was not just a celebration of tradition, but a celebration of belonging itself.

By the time the evening drew to a close, Aaryan felt a profound sense of connection. The apartment, once just walls and furniture, had become a gathering place, a bridge between cultures, and a space where differences were acknowledged and celebrated rather than feared or ignored. He noticed small gestures, the way a guest helped carry a dish, how laughter bounced from one corner to another, how Leila explained the decorations with pride, that together created an unspoken language of community.

As he cleaned up afterward, stacking plates and wiping down counters, he felt gratitude for the journey. The uncertainty, the missteps, the language struggles, and the cultural misreads had not vanished, but they had transformed. They had become lessons, building blocks that allowed him to engage, contribute, and belong. In his mind, he promised himself to continue bridging worlds, sharing his heritage, learning theirs, and finding joy in the ongoing conversation that life in this country offered.

That night, as he lay in bed reflecting on the day, he realized that the games, the food, the decorations, and the laughter were symbols of something far deeper: a life rebuilt, a sense of self reaffirmed, and the quiet power of human connection that transcends language, nationality, and past hardships. He felt at home, not because everything was familiar, but because he had created familiarity through participation, empathy, and care.

Aaryan understood that belonging was not a destination, but a process. This Thanksgiving marked a milestone in his journey, a testament to patience, effort, and openness. He knew challenges would continue to come, but he also knew that with courage, dedication, and the willingness to engage, he could navigate the unfamiliar, create bridges, and celebrate both his roots and his present with equal pride.

CHAPTER NINE

# Path to Success

The factory floor hummed with the rhythmic drone of machinery, the metallic clang of tools echoing through the cavernous hall. Aaryan wiped the sweat from his brow, feeling the sting of the harsh fluorescent lights overhead. He moved swiftly along the assembly line, performing the same repetitive tasks he had grown accustomed to over the past months. Colleagues glanced at him occasionally, some with admiration, others with casual indifference, as the supervisor's voice barked orders over the din. It was a world of precision and monotony, a place where mistakes were costly, and efficiency was measured every second.

For a moment, Aaryan paused, his hands resting on the cold metal of the workstation. He had reached a milestone recently, earning the 'Employee of the Month' recognition for his dedication and speed. The certificate, small and laminated, sat in the corner of his shared locker, a symbol of acknowledgment for hours of meticulous work. Yet, as he traced his fingers along the edges, a quiet unease stirred within him. The accolade, though validating, felt incomplete. He knew, with a clarity that refused to be ignored, that the factory had become a ceiling rather than a launchpad. The work sharpened his attention and built endurance, but it did little to stretch his mind or craft the professional life he aspired to.

He glanced around at the bustling machines, the synchronized movements of his coworkers, and the endless repetition of parts moving along the line. He could not deny the pride in being recognized, but he also could not ignore the gnawing thought that he had more to give, more to achieve. Aaryan's ambitions extended far beyond the walls of the factory.

He envisioned a future in which his ideas, his creativity, and his drive were not confined to mechanical precision but directed toward building solutions, creating value, and contributing in ways that challenged him intellectually.

The evening shift pressed on, and with each passing hour, the restlessness inside him grew. He had come here to work, yes, but he also came to grow. He wanted to rise beyond simple tasks and predictable routines. Sitting in the break room, sipping lukewarm coffee and listening to the low chatter of his colleagues, he allowed himself a rare moment of reflection. The recognition of his current achievement did not diminish the truth that he needed more. His mind traced the contours of his aspirations, the vision of a career that intertwined passion, innovation, and purpose. The factory had provided him with a foundation, but it was time to leap.

By the time the whistle signaled the end of the shift, Aaryan had made a decision. He would pursue an opportunity that demanded less immediate comfort and security but promised the growth he craved. There was a technology firm not far from the city center offering an internship in software development. The pay was modest, far below what he earned at the factory, but the experience promised exposure, mentorship, and a pathway into a field that fascinated him. He felt the familiar rush of excitement mingled with trepidation. Taking a step backward in terms of immediate earnings was not easy. It required a leap of faith, a willingness to sacrifice the present for a future that gleamed with possibility.

That evening, he drafted a careful email to the HR manager at the tech company, attaching his résumé and outlining his motivation for joining as an intern. Each word felt weighty, a declaration of intent that carried the full force of his ambition. Hitting send, he felt a surge of adrenaline and a pang of uncertainty, a duality he had come to recognize as part of pursuing something meaningful.

The next day, he approached his supervisor with a mixture of determination and humility. "Sir, I wanted to speak with you about an opportunity I have," he began, choosing his words carefully. His supervisor, a seasoned man with a commanding presence and an appreciation for diligence, raised an eyebrow. Aaryan explained that he had been offered an internship in technology, a field he had long desired to explore, and that he had decided to accept it.

The response was immediate and layered. "Aaryan, we value your work here. You are one of the best on this line. Losing you would be a setback for the team. Are you sure this is what you want? We can get you a raise if money is the problem." His supervisor's tone balanced concern and authority, a voice honed over years of managing efficiency and productivity.

Aaryan nodded firmly, meeting the gaze of the man who had come to respect his dedication. "No. No, sir. I am not leaving for money. I am grateful for everything I have learned here, but I need to grow. This is the step I have to take for my future."

The conversation was not easy. His supervisor outlined alternatives, promises of raises, and additional responsibilities that would place him at the top of the factory's hierarchy. Aaryan listened, appreciating the gesture and the recognition it represented, but the allure of remaining in a role that no longer challenged him could not compete with the vision he held for himself. He thanked his supervisor sincerely, expressing gratitude for mentorship and camaraderie, then formalized his resignation, leaving the factory with a mixture of relief, nostalgia, and anticipation.

The days that followed were a blend of preparation and reflection. Aaryan spent evenings brushing up on coding exercises, reviewing online tutorials, and familiarizing himself with the tools and workflows he would encounter during the internship. Each night, he allowed himself a quiet acknowledgment of the dichotomy he had just navigated: leaving behind comfort and recognition for uncertainty, leaving behind validation for potential. It was a choice rooted in vision rather than fear, in ambition rather than complacency.

When his first day at the tech company arrived, Aaryan walked into the office with a sense of purpose he had not felt in months. The air smelled faintly of coffee and electronics, a sharp contrast to the oily scent of the factory. The open space was bright and airy. Screens glowed with lines of code, emails, and charts. People moved quickly, discussing tasks in voices that were calm but precise, typing fast, pointing at monitors, sketching diagrams on whiteboards. Everything seemed to happen at a pace he had never experienced before, and for a moment, he felt the old knot of fear return.

"Good morning! You must be Aaryan," said a woman with short hair and glasses, holding out her hand. "I'm Jessica. I'll be showing you around today."

"Good morning," he said, shaking her hand. His voice felt a little small in the room filled with tapping keyboards and chatter.

Jessica led him to a workstation at the far end, near two large monitors. "This will be your desk. Today, we'll start with a small project. Don't worry, nothing too complicated. It's just a debugging task."

Aaryan nodded, though the word "debugging" carried both excitement and anxiety. He had studied programming, read tutorials, and done small exercises, but this was real code—lines written by other people, part of a live system that mattered to the company.

He opened the project folder and stared at the screen. Hundreds of lines of code scrolled past him. Functions nested within other functions, variables with names he had to double-check, syntax he had to parse carefully. His first task was to find why a small feature in the application wasn't working—why a button click didn't produce the expected output.

"Look at this function," Jessica said, pointing at a section of JavaScript code. "This is where the problem probably lies. Try adding some console logs and see what happens."

Aaryan's fingers hovered over the keyboard. "Console logs… okay," he muttered. He typed carefully, adding lines of code to print out values at different stages. The first run failed; nothing worked as expected. The red error messages glared at him.

"Don't stress it," Jessica said, leaning over. "It happens to everyone. Let's look together."

They went line by line, reading variables, checking conditions. Aaryan learned quickly that programming wasn't just about typing commands; it was about thinking in sequences, anticipating what the system was doing at every step. Hours passed in this focused silence. He scribbled notes on a pad, wrote down terms he didn't fully understand, like asynchronous callbacks and event loops, and asked questions whenever he could.

"Why does this run first, even though I called this function later?" he asked, pointing at a small snippet of code.

Jessica smiled. "Ah, that's because it's asynchronous. Some things run in the background while other things continue. It's tricky at first. Just keep experimenting, you'll get it."

By mid-morning, Aaryan felt a spark of understanding. The logs now displayed values as expected, and slowly, the button began to respond. It wasn't perfect, but it worked. A tiny triumph, a quiet surge of confidence. He leaned back in his chair and exhaled, the red warnings replaced by green success messages.

Later, he attended his first team meeting. Everyone sat around a large table, laptops open, notepads ready. Ideas flew quickly, how to improve features, fix bugs, optimize performance. At first, Aaryan stayed quiet, taking notes, trying to keep up with the terms: API, database, front-end, back-end, push request, merge conflicts. The words sometimes made sense, sometimes bounced past him.

After a while, one of the engineers, a young man named Carlos, asked him, "Aaryan, do you have any thoughts on how we might handle this form validation issue?"

Aaryan hesitated. His mind raced. He had seen similar examples in tutorials but never in a real system. Slowly, he said, "Maybe… we could check the input values before sending them to the server? That might prevent errors earlier."

"Exactly!" Carlos said, smiling. "That's one way. Good thinking."

The small recognition made him feel grounded, like he belonged there. It wasn't just about coding—it was about thinking logically, noticing patterns, suggesting solutions.

After the meeting, Aaryan walked back to his desk, his mind buzzing with new terms, diagrams, and snippets of conversation he was only beginning to understand. For the first time in weeks, he allowed himself a small smile. The work was different. Mentally demanding, yes, but lighter on the body than the long hours in the warehouse or factory. The hum of machinery, the ache in his arms, the constant physical rhythm—he realized he would not miss it, not in this way.

Yet even as he welcomed the change, a quiet nostalgia settled over him. He thought of the factory floor, the familiar faces of colleagues who had become part of his routine, the small victories of efficiency, the camaraderie forged in shared labor. That work had been hard, repetitive, but it had also grounded him. It had given him a sense of accomplishment, tangible in calloused hands and finished tasks. That chapter of his life felt like a core memory, one he would carry with a strange mixture of pride and longing.

Still, he knew that this new job offered something different: a path out of his current living situation, a chance to secure a stable income, and an opportunity to build toward independence. The cramped room he now called home, the small bed, the table with peeling paint, the single window staring at the brick wall, felt more like a temporary station than a home. With better pay and steady work, he could imagine moving somewhere of his own, creating a space that reflected him rather than necessity.

He looked out the window at the city stretching beyond the office, its rhythm pulsing through him. This new job was an unfamiliar language, a different kind of challenge, but it held promise. It was not only a step toward financial freedom and independence; it was an opportunity to reframe his identity, to see himself not just as a worker struggling to survive, but as a thinker, a learner, someone capable of building more than just a day-to-day existence.

For the first time in months, Aaryan felt lively and hopeful. The house that had sheltered him, cramped and full of memories, would always be part of him, but now it seemed possible to move forward, to carve out a life that balanced the warmth of the past with the promise of what lay ahead.

The week continued in the same pattern: small debugging tasks, attending meetings, reading documentation, asking questions, sometimes making mistakes. He accidentally deleted a test file and had to apologize and recover it. Another time, he misread a variable name and spent an hour tracking down the problem. Each error frustrated him, but he also learned something every time: attention to detail, the importance of asking questions, patience, and perseverance.

By Friday, he could see the progress. Tasks that had seemed impossible on Monday now felt manageable. He could read code without stopping at every line, he could understand error messages more clearly, and he could contribute small suggestions in meetings. His hands typed faster, his thoughts lined up more clearly, and each tiny success built confidence.

Sitting at his desk Friday evening, he looked at the screen. The first week had ended. His code had been reviewed, corrected, accepted. He realized that what had seemed overwhelming—the complexity, the technical jargon, the pressure to perform—was manageable if he approached it piece by piece. One function at a time, one problem at a time. He reflected on the factory work, the repetitive physical labor, the rhythm of machines. That had taught him discipline and endurance. This new environment demanded mental endurance and precision, and he was learning it, slowly but surely.

Aaryan leaned back in his chair, stretching his arms, and smiled softly. It was not a dramatic victory, not a moment of fireworks. It was subtle, internal. The kind of triumph that whispered, *You belong here. You can learn. You can grow.* And for him, it was enough.

He shut down his computer, gathered his things, and walked toward the elevator. The hum of the office faded behind him, replaced by the city sounds outside. The weekend awaited, but so did the anticipation of Monday. Aaryan knew he had entered a space that challenged him, pushed him, and made him rethink his limits. And for the first time in months, he treated himself to a luxurious fine dining.

Week after week, Aaryan leaned into his learning, asking questions, seeking clarification, and absorbing the guidance offered by his mentors in the company. He reminded himself that the discomfort was a sign of growth, that the uncertainty he felt was a necessary companion to the aspirations he sought to realize. He recalled every late night spent learning programming basics, every small success in mastering syntax and logic, and he drew strength from the cumulative effort that had brought him to this moment.

Just a month into the internship, Aaryan began to notice subtle transformations. Tasks that once seemed insurmountable became manageable. Confidence in participating during discussions grew, and he started proposing small ideas and improvements. The sense of fulfillment derived from tackling complex problems ignited a drive he had not experienced while working in the factory. Each challenge he overcame strengthened his belief that he belonged in this field, that the sacrifices he had made were worth the pursuit of long-term growth over short-term comfort.

He also found moments of camaraderie among fellow interns and mentors, connections that reminded him of the importance of community in professional development. Lunches turned into conversations about strategy, coding techniques, and future aspirations. The shared pursuit of knowledge fostered a sense of belonging and reinforced the notion that growth is rarely solitary. The work environment, demanding and dynamic, became a place of learning, mentorship, and opportunity—a stark contrast to the routine he had left behind.

Aaryan's journey in this chapter of his life was defined not by immediate recognition or accolades but by the intentional pursuit of advancement, the courage to leave security behind, and the willingness to embrace challenges that promised skill, insight, and professional expansion. The lessons he carried were clear: fulfillment lies not in accolades alone but in the spaces where one is tested, where effort meets opportunity, and where the vision of a future self drives every decision in the present.

By the end of his first month, Aaryan recognized the significance of his choice. He had left behind a role in which he excelled, traded comfort for growth, and chosen a path that demanded learning, resilience, and patience. The factory and its accolades remained part of his story, but they no longer defined him. With renewed focus, he embraced the internship with passion and drive, understanding that the steps he was taking now were laying the foundation for the professional life he envisioned—one built on knowledge, creativity, and the courage to pursue opportunity over ease.

CHAPTER TEN

# Reflections on the Journey

Sitting by the window of his small apartment, Aaryan watched the city hum with life. The cars, the chatter, the distant sound of sirens and laughter—all of it felt like a pulse, a rhythm he had learned to follow over the past year. Yet even as the world moved outside, his mind drifted back to the India he had left behind. The contrast was striking. Back home, streets were alive in a different way. People spoke loudly, collided in markets, and somehow found joy in chaos. Here, even when the streets were crowded, there was a sense of separation, of personal space that sometimes felt isolating.

He thought about his first months in this country, when every interaction was a small test. Ordering a simple coffee could take minutes of hesitation and repeated attempts. Conversations in the office required translating his thoughts into careful English. He remembered standing in line at the grocery store, rehearsing words in his head, only to stumble over them when it was his turn. He had learned patience, and he had learned resilience, but he had also learned how lonely it could feel to exist in a place where your voice did not carry the weight it once did.

Aaryan remembered a conversation with Ravi during one of their weekend check-ins. He had confessed his frustration over a missed promotion, his inability to send money home, and his fear of stagnation.

"I feel invisible sometimes," he had said, voice low. "I work hard, I try, but I am not enough here."

Ravi had leaned back in his chair, looking thoughtful. "You are learning," he said slowly. "And learning is not about being perfect. It is about building value, bit by bit. People notice, even when you think they do not."

That conversation had stayed with him. Aaryan realized that the journey was not just about physical distance, but about internal recalibration. He had moved continents, but he had also moved into a new version of himself. A version that could endure uncertainty, confront fear, and build skills not just for survival, but for growth.

He thought about his language classes with Fatima. At first, he had gone reluctantly, doubting he could ever communicate fluently. But the patience and warmth she had shown had shifted something in him. Sitting in a room with people who were also strangers in a foreign land, all fumbling through words and stories, had taught him humility. It had taught him that connection did not require perfection. Small gestures—a smile, a laugh, a nod of understanding—could bridge gaps far wider than language alone.

Leila's presence in those early days had also left an imprint. She had been a spark, an example of openness and enthusiasm. Even in moments of self-doubt, her belief in him had reminded him that connection was a two-way street. He recalled her teasing him over the misaligned pie crust at the Thanksgiving preparation, how she had laughed, not to mock, but to encourage. Those moments of lightness had carried weight.

Aaryan reflected on the blog he had started months ago, and the community that had grown around it. What had begun as a personal outlet for his experiences and frustrations had blossomed into a platform where voices from across the country and even abroad converged. Immigrants shared their struggles, their triumphs, and their ordinary yet extraordinary moments. For the first time, he felt part of a larger conversation, a network that validated his feelings while also teaching him about resilience, empathy, and shared humanity. He smiled as he remembered a reader from Texas who wrote about navigating their first winter alone, and another from Canada who shared memories of Diwali in a snowy cityscape. Those stories became threads weaving together the sense of community he had once sought so desperately in real life.

There were, of course, contradictions in his experience. He had become comfortable navigating cultural norms, yet he could not shake the moments of dissonance. Football games with colleagues, conversations about pop culture, jokes that flew over his head—these were daily reminders that belonging was layered and uneven. Even when invited to dinners or social outings, there remained the subtle awareness of being an outsider, of translating not just words but entire ways of thinking. It was exhausting at times, and he often questioned whether his efforts were noticed or appreciated.

Yet those contradictions also fueled his reflections. He began to see patterns in the immigrant experience that he had once dismissed as personal struggles. The lack of collectivity, the insistence on individual success, the thin veneer of neighborly connection, even in small towns, spoke to cultural differences that shaped his life in ways he could not ignore. While in India, community was often tangible—shared meals, festivals in streets, neighbors who looked out for each other—here, independence came with distance. People were polite but rarely engaged deeply without reason. That realization stung, yet it also gave him clarity. He could not control society, but he could create small spaces of engagement, inclusion, and understanding, like his blog, the Thanksgiving dinner, and his participation in community events.

He thought about the setbacks, particularly the job loss and financial strain that had made him question his value. At the time, it had felt catastrophic. Unable to send money home, unable to measure himself against the standards he had carried since childhood, he had faced the raw weight of responsibility. But those moments had also clarified his priorities. He had learned to focus on skill-building, to become invaluable in ways that transcended his initial roles. He remembered nights spent studying, practicing presentations, improving English, and volunteering. The small victories accumulated into tangible progress, each one quietly affirming that persistence could shift outcomes.

Aaryan sighed and leaned back, thinking of the life he had built. He had discovered that belonging was not a state granted by society, but a space cultivated by effort and courage. It was in the conversations at community centers, the laughter during dinners, the shared curiosity at games, and the written words that connected strangers across miles. It was in the willingness to make mistakes, to speak imperfectly, and to try again.

He remembered a particular morning when he posted a reflective blog entry about celebrating Diwali alone in his apartment, including a small virtual call with friends from back home. Comments flooded in, sharing similar experiences and offering empathy. The sense of resonance was profound. He realized that the immigrant journey was as much about connecting hearts as it was about learning norms. Sharing stories, celebrating successes, and acknowledging hardships—it was these acts that built belonging.

Aaryan's thoughts wandered to the future. There were still uncertainties: career shifts, potential moves, family needs, and cultural adaptation. But the fear that had once dominated his every thought had diminished. It had been replaced by confidence tempered with humility, pride mixed with reflection. He understood now that life's value did not come solely from achievement, but from engagement, from the willingness to show up, and from the conscious effort to build bridges across difference.

He whispered quietly to himself, almost as if testing the words: "I am here. I am part of something. I belong."

The reflection was not celebratory in a naive sense. It was honest, acknowledging pain, dislocation, and failure while also embracing growth, connection, and agency. Aaryan understood the contradictions: the nostalgia for home versus the joy of independence, the gaps in understanding versus the depth of learning, the distance from community versus the bonds he had intentionally built. Each tension was part of the fabric of his life abroad, a life that he now claimed not just for survival, but for meaning.

As evening descended, Aaryan opened his laptop and began to draft a new blog post. He wrote about gratitude for the lessons learned, the people who had guided him, and the courage it took to show up every day. He included reflections on cultural dissonance, the challenges of building skills, and the quiet victories that often went unnoticed. He wanted readers to feel both the rawness of struggle and the hope of growth, to understand that moving across continents was more than a change of address—it was a transformation of self.

The words flowed more easily than they ever had before. Each sentence carried weight because it was lived, not imagined. Each paragraph became a mirror of experience, capturing not just a story of one man but a reflection of countless others navigating new lands. When he paused to look out the window again, the city lights glimmered in the distance. Aaryan felt the simultaneous ache of longing and the steady pulse of belonging. The journey from India to here had been long, uneven, and painful. Yet in that moment, he recognized that he had arrived—not at a place, but at a version of himself capable of understanding, bridging, and creating.

The room was quiet except for the faint tapping of the keyboard and the occasional hum from the street below. Aaryan allowed himself to feel the magnitude of the path he had taken, and he smiled softly. He had crossed oceans and fears alike. He had confronted failure, loneliness, and doubt. And through it all, he had built a life that was his own, one rooted in reflection, empathy, and action. The world outside continued its rhythm, but for the first time, he felt not just a participant, but a composer of his own narrative.

www.ingramcontent.com/pod-product-compliance
Ingram Content Group UK Ltd.
Pitfield, Milton Keynes, MK11 3LW, UK
UKHW041317190726
13845UKWH00025B/339

9 789355 926494